THE TERROR OF EVIDENCE

UNTIMELY MEDITATIONS

THE TERROR OF EVIDENCE

MARCUS STEINWEG

FOREWORD BY THOMAS HIRSCHHORN

TRANSLATED BY AMANDA DEMARCO

THE MIT PRESS
CAMBRIDGE, MASSACHUSETTS
LONDON, ENGLAND

Originally published as *Evidenzterror* in the series *Fröhliche Wissenschaft* by Matthes & Seitz Berlin: © Matthes & Seitz Berlin Verlagsgesellschaft mbH, Berlin 2015. All rights reserved.

This book was set in PF Din Text Pro by Toppan Best-set Premedia Limited.

Library of Congress Cataloging-in-Publication Data

Names: Steinweg, Marcus, 1971- author. | DeMarco, Amanda, author.
Title: The terror of evidence / Marcus Steinweg ; foreword by Thomas Hirschhorn ; translated by Amanda DeMarco.
Other titles: Evidenzterror. English
Description: Cambridge, MA : MIT Press, [2017] | Series: Untimely meditations | Includes bibliographical references.
Identifiers: LCCN 2016034154 | ISBN 9780262533430 (pbk. : alk. paper)
Subjects: LCSH: Philosophy and civilization. | Arts--Philosophy.
Classification: LCC B59 .S7413 2017 | DDC 190--dc23 LC record available at https://lccn.loc.gov/2016034154

Deux excès: exclure la raison, n'admettre que la raison.

—BLAISE PASCAL

CONTENTS

Marcus Steinweg's Hardcore Thinking—with a Light Heart

One day during summer 2013 at Forest Houses in the South Bronx, at the *Gramsci Monument* where Marcus Steinweg held seventy-seven "Daily Philosophical Lectures," titled: "How to Be Critical?," "What Is Truth?," "Romantic Shit," or "What Does It Mean to Be a Philosopher Today?," one of the residents—a daily visitor of the *Gramsci Monument*—stood up and addressed him: "How can you, Marcus, declare 'God is dead' to us for whom religion is important, to us who need religion in our daily lives?" Serious and calm, Marcus Steinweg answered how important, even crucial, it is to him—as a philosopher—to think without safeguards and without religion. How important it is to him—as a philosopher—to understand thinking as an act of losing one's grip and how philosophy needs to be an act of absolute freedom beyond ideology or dogma. He explained that thinking's only chance to go beyond an opportunistic idea, simplified opinion or reductive ideology is by including overcomplexity and vulnerability. He explained that "God is dead" means that the absolute Judge, the one who designates the guilty, is "dead." It's a matter not of guilt but of responsibility. He explained that real thinking has no certitude, no comfort or guaranty. "God is dead" doesn't mean that there is no meaning; rather, what used to be unique has been replaced by an overwhelming amount of meanings. Meaning is no longer single and solid; it has become a construction of thousands of safeguards. And philosophers can't use safeguards, he insisted. The daily visitor understood his point immediately and remained truthful and engaged to the very last lecture.

This anecdote points out the power and radicalism of Marcus Steinweg's thinking, his sovereignty in his practice of philosophy and his self-understanding as a philosopher. His capacity to implicate the other is beautiful, bright, precise, and logical, grounded in everyday questions, which to him are always big questions. Speaking sharply and generously, Marcus Steinweg has the knowledge and credibility that can make someone—actually anyone—love philosophy, just because he loves it himself. He has the charisma to reach the Other, the one who—perhaps—does not understand, the one who is skeptical, the one who still doubts. Marcus Steinweg is able to share this passion every day, every moment, under any circumstance—with and for the Other. I have known Marcus Steinweg since 1998, when we met in Cologne during the preparation of my exhibition "Rolex etc., Freundlich's 'Aufstieg' und Skulptur-Sortier-Station-Dokumentation" at Museum Ludwig. We became friends, and I invited him to contribute lectures and texts to many projects of mine such as *Bataille Monument*, *Swiss Swiss-Democracy*, *24h Foucault*, or *The Bijlmer Spinoza-Festival*. His commitment and engagement to make philosophy the core—the hardcore—of life reflects his competence, and its outcome is and will be important for him, for me, and for philosophy and the history of philosophy.

Marcus Steinweg and I together created the notion of "Friendship between Art and Philosophy." This idea is based on the conviction that art and philosophy are movements that reach beyond the historical moment in which they were conceived. Art and philosophy share notions such as "headlessness," "resistance," "courage," and "hope," and interrogations such as "How to give form?," "How to conceive a concept?," "How to create truth?," and "How to create a universal truth?" "Friendship between Art and Philosophy" keeps the fire going, and we keep the flame alive. Friendship also means learning from each other. I learned about the absolute love of philosophy—or art—and how this love can determine all decisions. Art and philosophy sometimes share similar dynamics, graceful moments of encounters in concepts and forms. I learned from Marcus Steinweg that— as a philosopher and as an artist—we have to be ready and always first to pay the price for our work, for our thoughts, for our position, for our form. I learned from him not to be disappointed by reality—that, to the contrary, the "disappointing" reality must absolutely be the field where thinking, forging a position, and giving form must be asserted in a gesture of emancipation. I learned from Marcus Steinweg that "nonsense" is important, not as counterpoint to "sense" but as "nonsense" in itself. I witnessed at the *Gramsci Monument* and at numerous other venues that, through thinking, Marcus Steinweg's philosophy can reach the nonexclusive, can touch the universe, can interrogate the other , and finally can implicate him.

In the book you hold in your hands the aphorisms reflect the same clarity, exactitude, and evidence of Marcus Steinweg's inclusive and therefore outstanding way of explaining his concepts. This book is a kind of lexicon or atlas of terms such as "sex," "desubjectivation," "misunderstanding." The table of contents is in itself excessive and ambitious. It invites me, as reader, to find terms that interest me, or I can turn to any page randomly or use my own search criteria. All terms float freely like single verses of a never-ending poem. Nothing is simplified or abbreviated. Every term is new and enlightened in its own singularity, in its density, explosiveness, and charge. As an artist, to read Marcus Steinweg's definition of art—"To respond to the no-form with form, without neutralizing it"—is wonderful and truly helpful. The philosopher breaks, hammers, grinds what is not essential, what is not crucial, always insisting with the hypercomplexity and malleability of each term. Marcus Steinweg builds a sculpture, a sculpture of notions, never finished yet active, dynamic, and always moving. He sets fire and ignites an acceleration that urges me to think more, to think more clearly, to think more powerfully, to think faster, to think beyond. Marcus Steinweg's hardcore philosophy compels me to think with a light heart and to think for myself. What could be more beautiful?

Thomas Hirschhorn
Aubervilliers, 2016

THE TERROR OF EVIDENCE

OWL

One old notion of thought conceives of it as a man bent over the objects of his cognition, as over a corpse. He only manages to think what is dead. All that is living resists his impulse to confine things into categories and concepts. It eludes the gaze of the luckless subject, who only manages to glimpse traces of its absence. The correlation of thought and being or subject and object describes the drama of a living being who, by beginning to think them, kills the object of his thought. What he ultimately holds in his hands or retains as an object is a dead body that hardly bears a resemblance to the intended object. Is to think to kill, then? Does thinking bury what is thought by hastening it to its grave? We've grown accustomed to the fact that belatedness is inherent to thought: "The owl of Minerva spreads its wings only with the falling of dusk."[1] It is philosophy's bird of death. But what if, more than killing through belatedness, creation through anteriority is inherent to thought? It's not as if thought kills or creates the object of its recognition in the act of recognition. Thinking means abandoning oneself to an experience of acceleration that carries the subject beyond its objects. It does not produce them. It draws them in its direction by being located where there is not already an object. That is the empty space between the present and the future—the space in which what Gilles Deleuze called *becoming* occurs. Beyond history, in the midst of history. The deaf, sightless, dumb heart of reality. In Hegel's owl, we must welcome the bird of a present whose faceless truth explodes every present. Thinking means not only preparing for and witnessing this explosion. Thinking means carrying it out.

PATHOS

Thinking that thinks itself—the self-reflection of the logos, the cogito, or the subject—implies the veritable pathos of reason. There is no doctrine of reason that is not a doctrine of emotion. The reasoning subject cannot think itself without being confronted with its own fragmentation, the pain that belongs to self-awareness.[2] The Ancient Greek verb *páschein* means *to suffer* or *to endure*—and what is suffering other than an experience that pushes the subject to its limits? Pathos expresses the experience of unresolvable conflict, which is why there is no philosophy that isn't pathetic in this sense. It may be a matter of the discreet pathos of mathematical thinking, or lines of argument strained to their breaking point. It may be the polemic pathos of reason run riot, which we are familiar with from Nietzsche's final books and Artaud's strident invectives (from his "animalistic and superhuman, shrieking, shrill, brutal" speech).[3] The pathos of dry subjects, abstraction, sobriety, and coldness also expresses the pain of thought, in which it "loses itself," as Hegel says.[4] Thinking means getting lost again and again. The self grinds itself down on its conflicts instead of synthesizing them dialectically. The movement of reason traces its restlessness. Thinking is a passion that makes the subject tremble in the face of truths that undermine its realities.

MARCUS STEINWEG

PHILOSOPHY

You might define philosophy as an answer to the question *What is philosophy?* That doesn't mean that there's a final answer. On the contrary, it means that such an answer will never come, and that the impossibility of a conclusive answer to the question contributes to its answer. It's a question that poses itself again and again. You can't philosophize without being confronted with this question, being goaded on by it, emboldened, and unnerved. It's what keeps philosophical thought on edge. Not only does the question arise from the heart of philosophy, but the possibilities for answering it are also ignited there. Michel Foucault said the same thing about literature: "'What is literature?' is neither the question of a critic nor of a historian nor a sociologist contemplating a particular linguistic issue. There is a sort of hollowness inside literature, in which it itself finally takes its place and in which its entire being is probably contained."[5] The same is true of philosophy. Historians of science, cultural theorists, and sociologists all have an external view of a practice in which they themselves hardly participate. They dedicate themselves to it like a zoologist to an exotic animal. The study and analysis of the conditions of philosophical thought, its historical framework, and the way it is situated politically are just a part of the activity known as philosophy. They correlate with an external gaze, similar to the gaze of the anatomist or pathologist, straining for objectivity. The question of what philosophy is cannot be answered from that standpoint, but the question of what is proper to it can be. It's important to distinguish between the two questions—not to attribute a transhistorical substance to philosophy, but to wrest it from the disciples of fact-esotericism and their pseudo-substantialism. Philosophy is precisely that: rebellion against the facts, resistance to the "cult of the 'realities,'"[6] and impassioned challenging of historicism and faith in information. The problematic thing about these forms of realism is that they are actually forms of idealism. Every serious philosopher—be it Spinoza, Kant, Hegel, Schopenhauer, Husserl, Heidegger, Wittgenstein, Adorno, Weil, Lacan, Foucault, Deleuze, Cavell, Derrida, Badiou, Kittler, Nancy, Agamben, Žižek, or Butler—knows that the question of what philosophy is can be answered only when the false dichotomy between realism and idealism is discarded. True idealism defies fact-esotericism, in that it is oriented toward a reality beyond esotericism's horizon. True realism circumscribes idealistic escapism with a kind of thought that recognizes immanent transcendence.[7] And the fools want to see that as a regression into metaphysics and religion. They don't comprehend that what they take for metaphysics survived on the terrain of the most prosaic positivism, in the form of a fact-obscurantism that corresponds to the stance of the last man in Nietzsche's *Zarathustra*. Nothing protects the stupid from their stupidity—not even not having read Nietzsche, not having burned their fingers on him. Inherent to philosophy is resistance to the active nonthought that I call stupidity. It is a resistance that does not exhaust itself in negativism. It

MARCUS STEINWEG

implies the self-propulsion of the thinking subject as it makes its way to the point of inconsistency between its realities. In this subject, the will to investigate the edges of its world finds its expression. Neither the juridical posture of the critic nor the professorial arrogance of the academic makes you a philosopher. After all, philosophers inhabit the world by withdrawing their trust from it. They live in a reality that is devoid of any evidence.[8] Thinking means coping with this lack of evidence. It reveals itself most clearly at the points where the promise of consistency is boundless. One initial answer to the question *What is philosophy?* could be: philosophy is the experience of inconsistency as a way of life.

HOUSE

Metaphors of architecture pervade Western thought, from Plato's Cave to Descartes's *fundamentum inconcussum* to Heidegger's talk of language as the "house of being"[9] and Foucault's evocation of the "great Platonic building of thought."[10] The houses of philosophy need not be palaces. Hegel's systems are reminiscent of cathedrals or skyscrapers; Nietzsche's collections of aphorisms reminiscent of nomadic tent cities; Luhmann's systems theory models reminiscent of gigantic office complexes—and they're all planted out in the emptiness and built on sand! Philosophers build their homes in the desert; they board ships to traverse entire oceans with them as if they were floating houses. There are more modest architectures—the third-generation Frankfurt School's row houses, to name one. Heidegger's predilection for huts expresses not modesty but rather the pathos of a monkish existence. Show me how someone builds and I will tell you how they think. Take the Wittgenstein House in Vienna's third district, for example. There are academic discourses whose structure, language, and line of argumentation resemble the place of their production and teaching: consider the democratic, functional architecture of universities, with their polished floors and hallways. Derrida's lectures remind us of grandiose theaters, while Foucault's heterotopias (hospitals, prisons, etc.) influence his textual topologies; the great books by Deleuze are hysterical concept-architectures; together with their statistics, Bourdieu's sociological analyses have the charm of industrial buildings; Badiou constructs his ideas mathematically; Agamben proceeds as meticulously as the master builders of antiquity. They're all concerned with structural engineering and load-bearing capacity. Everyone is asking themselves if what they're building will hold up. They're still seeking a foundation for their constructions long after they've begun to doubt its existence. The fact that God is dead means that there is no one absolute architect. And philosophers are by no means suitable replacements. They build in the shadow of his absence. The Greek word *oikos* can be translated as *house* or *tomb*. The houses of the philosophers are also burial grounds. Dead gods haunt them like ghosts. Thought will never be anything more than the archiving of this ghost.

MARCUS STEINWEG

COURBET

The French noun *immensité* is mainly used as an adjective in English, or perhaps as a descriptive substantive ("the immensity of the problem"), but it rarely stands independently. The immense—that's something you don't hear very often. We speak of immense resources or immense effort without thinking twice. In 1869, Gustave Courbet titled a famous painting *L'immensité*. It shows what can only be shown but not depicted: the infinite. The *immensité*, the immense, designates something that exceeds all measure. It is related to the incommensurable, the lack of a common scale between two or more magnitudes. *Immense* and *incommensurable* are words that point to the gigantic, which can also be inconceivably small. Of course, this vocabulary sets us on the trail of the sublime or the exalted. The critical question is how to shift this vocabulary into the horizon of an immanence that knows no alternative— that is, to locate it precisely where it has lost its right to remain or exist. Courbet's painterly materialism—which anticipates what Foucault recognized in Manet: the full exploitation of the signifiers, the canvas, the oil paint in its material substance, and so on[11]—assigns itself this task, which marks one of contemporary philosophy's most important problems: When working under conditions of heightened finiteness, how do we salvage the infinite? How do we conceive of the immense and the infinite in the context of their desublimation and detheologization? And finally, when operating within the horizon of radical materialism, how do we prevent it from regressing into idealism while remaining committed to scrutinizing its consistency or inconsistency?

CLUB SANDWICH

Michel Foucault's love of American cuisine is well known: "A good club sandwich with a coke. That's my pleasure. It's true. With ice cream."[12] Doesn't that fit just perfectly with Gilles Deleuze's love of American literature? Here, the affirmation of deterritorialization—the Nietzschean affirmation of contingency that repudiates ancestral Europeanism with its worship of the past, its metaphysics of interiority, its intimist psychology—follows a Hyperborean line to the exterior; there, a passion for surfaces and structuralism of the shallows culminates in an aesthetics of existence, replacing any traditionalism and every culture, even haute cuisine, with a *savoir vivre* (*technê tou biou*) that distances itself from its origins. Both combine affirmation with a motion that gives artificiality priority over nature. Both replace the metaphysics of origins with an open horizon.

TRAP

Kafka's "Little Fable" was first published in 1931:

> "Alas," said the mouse, "the world is growing smaller every day. At the beginning it was so big that I was afraid, I kept running and running, and I was glad when

MARCUS STEINWEG

at last I saw walls far away to the right and left, but these long walls have narrowed so quickly that I am in the last chamber already, and there in the corner stands the trap that I must run into."

"You only need to change your direction," said the cat, and ate it up.[13]

Before interpreting the text (which was titled and edited by Max Brod) to draw a moral from it whose evidence would annihilate it—that is, before caving in to the temptation of unambiguousness, which prattles on about the intractability of the human situation in order to activate the existential pathos of the absurd, while you hold forth about the most obvious interpretations—you could, though this is in all probability also a trap, glimpse in this story a trap that incites the reader to interpretations whose meaning gives up the text itself for lost.

ESCAPE

The dream of freedom, the "famous dream of unalienated man"[14] as Foucault describes it, brings the subject up against a boundary in order to awaken capacities within him that can hardly be called capacities for reason. Rather, contact with this boundary introduces the subject to the experience of impossible freedom, a freedom beyond freedom that articulates itself as the application of reason, the feverish act of self-transcendence by the human subject under an empty sky. Here, it begins to explore language as a means for articulating the unspeakable. In it, it discovers the medium for self-mediation without reason. Faced with the *animal rationale* that is the *zoon logon echon*—literally the "creature with a language"—nothing compels us to view it as an animal whose reason restrains its madness. The capacities for drift and losing the self are far more intrinsic to the speaking creature. Precisely here, in the element of language, it loses itself in its sheer insignificance. You can't claim that this loss of self only distances the subject from itself. Rather, the subject remains with itself in this distance from itself. Language becomes an escape from reason. No one has expressed this more beautifully than Foucault: "In a world where God is dead once and for all, and where we know, despite the promises from all sides, from the Right and from the Left, that we won't find happiness, language is our only resource, our only source. It reveals to us in the very hollow of our memories and beneath each of our words, beneath each of those words that gallop through our head, it reveals the majestic freedom of being mad."[15] Maybe one can say that using language opens a door for the human subject by familiarizing it with the limits of its reason. We have no grounds to speak of the romanticization of madness. The majestic freedom of being mad is part of the subject's normalcy.

SOAP BUBBLES

In the bursting of soap bubbles, our dreams burst, our hopes, illusions—that is, our *reality*. It would be naive to believe that our realities aren't soap bubbles. They have the same fragility and seductiveness. That doesn't mean that they have no substance at all and are nothing but chimeras. They're flying spheres, floating clouds, evanescing worlds like gliding orbs. Neither are they anchored to solid ground, nor do they metamorphose into some celestial substance. They're clouds of insubstantiality, which know only time and space, no earth and no sky. They are dream entities that emanate from our reason. But it's the sort of reason that can fly.

RESSENTIMENT

Nietzsche says of Napoleon, Goethe, Beethoven, Stendhal, Heinrich Heine, Schopenhauer, Richard Wagner, and Delacroix that their talent and their genius, their fanaticism and their impatience made them incapable of slowness. As he put it, subjects of an unconditional self-acceleration, which refuses to be restrained by any pragmatic considerations, are "incapable ... of a noble tempo, a *lento*."[16] They are too dominated by the will of expression. That makes them romantics of their desires, who, in their drivenness, make their will the gauge of necessity, which makes them deaf to the counsel of doxa. There's no reason to romanticize these romantics. It's enough to recognize them as such, even if they themselves—Goethe, for example—renounce romanticism. Ultimately it's not about romance, as long as we associate romance with a religiosity of longing. It's about pacing, precipitousness, and breathlessness. Artistic self-assertion means daring to make unsecured motions, having the courage to relinquish opportunities, risking doing what you're not capable of. That's why even today—in an era when we do everything to hold art's status as art against it, in order to emancipate ourselves from the ideology of the aesthetic—from all sides, every kind of art faces the accusation of insufficient seriousness. Basically, artists are accused of accelerating beyond the normal rate. They're accused of infractions of speed that make everyone who sticks to the speed limit look like an idiot. There's a word for the embarrassment of those left behind: *ressentiment*.

CONFINEMENT

Has anyone ever done more violence to *logos* than to confine it in the prison known as logic? And what if the speech, language, or reason known as logos were convicted of the inconsistency of its promise known as logic? Among heretics, an exactingness caused by excess is proper to thought, which tempts logos to break with its principles. Thinking means showing logos its own fragility.

MORTGAGE

The relationship between art and the critic is an expression of tension and difference. It's also a sibling relationship, because critical consciousness—as well as consciousness of the critical and its limits—belongs to art, which divests itself of acute evidence by demonstrating its own arbitrariness to it. At the same time, criticism takes a sort of loan

MARCUS STEINWEG

from art in order to be credibly critical instead of just a staging of the critical. Art must do the same, insofar as that means borrowing speculatively against its uncertain future. "As long as criticism is not an art alongside the other arts, it will remain petty, biased, unjust and trivial," Rilke once wrote.[17] Criticism is only critical when it is self-critical, which implies active self-destabilization. Its judgments are poised above myriad blind suppositions. It exists only as blind praxis based on a mortgage whose value goes undeclared.

LOYALTY THROUGH BETRAYAL

"One repays a teacher badly if one always remains a pupil only."[18]—In an era of infantilization in academic instruction, Nietzsche's statement is all the more relevant. The anti-authoritarianism of progressive thought—which is to say, every thought that does away with repetitive parroting in order to become a reinvention of the activity known as thinking—requires a break with the most obvious, most familiar, and most important concepts. It articulates itself as a break not just with the wrong, but also with the right and its self-righteous dominance. Derrida practiced it in many meticulous readings. To concede the utmost authority to a text by following its statements, idioms, and grammar into the most far-flung typographical corners, in order to reveal its inconsistencies and in this way to expose it a little, is what he called deconstruction: loyalty through betrayal—and vice versa!

HEBBEL WITH WITTGENSTEIN

The mutual compromising of belief and knowledge may find expression in the concept of the truth. In a diary entry from 1842, Friedrich Hebbel suggested this definition: "Truth is the point where belief and knowledge neutralize each other."[19] Truth allows neither knowledge nor belief to fully land the blow. It is the junction of both dimensions, theater of their encounter and their conflict. Knowledge would verify the truth of belief and, if not suspend it, at least restrain it. Belief can be experienced as the limitation, destabilization, and crutch of the truth of knowledge. "What I know, I believe,"[20] writes Ludwig Wittgenstein in *On Certainty*. That doesn't just mean that there is no knowledge without the prosthesis of belief. It also means that belief is a part of knowledge. In Hebbel's writings, you can deduce that the clashing and collaboration of belief and knowledge leads to a mutual neutralization in the very act of their alliance in order to produce a truth that eludes either individually.

REASON AS EXCESS

Marx wasn't the first to note the irrationality of reason. It already dominated the *Critique of Pure Reason* (1781/1787). You won't understand Kant if you don't take the title of the book seriously. What is *critique*? What sort of *purity* is being discussed? What does *reason* mean? And finally, what is this possessive construction trying to convey?

These questions can all be answered in brief. The critical faculty is the capacity to discriminate. It allows the subject, taking recourse to its transcendental condition, to discriminate between what it recognizes through sensory experiences and what marks the limits of its capacity for recognition by exceeding the sensory. Thought is critical if it recognizes the limits of reason. The purity of reason refers to its ability to detach itself from empiricism, to make judgments that are not based on experience and which therefore are not *a posteriori*, but rather *a priori*. Pure reason is reason that is independent of (direct) experience. Reason is not understanding. Whereas understanding represents the analytical capacity for categorical thought through the activation of forms of understanding (categories), reason raises the understanding subject above itself. In the Kantian sense, the entity known as reason short-circuits the human subject with its transcendent exterior, thus forming the irrational element of the human "disposition" (the unit of its transcendental capacities). It is precisely reason that articulates the excessive character of the subject. A critique of pure reason means that reason is the subject as well as the object of the procedure referred to as critique. The book's title sets the aporia-laden stage for disjointed subjectivity. This is already articulated in the first sentence of the preface to the first edition: "Human reason has the peculiar fate in one species of its cognitions that it is burdened with questions which it cannot dismiss, since they are given to it as problems by the nature of reason itself, but which it also cannot answer, since they transcend every capacity of human reason."[21] The second section of the book, "Transcendental Dialectic," which is dedicated to the paralogisms and antinomies of pure reason, essentially takes reason as the exemplary capacity for unreason. You can distill one of Kant's foundational messages into the following statement: the human subject is its own excess![22]

PLAY

"The entire endeavor of writing," according to Heiner Müller, aims at "reaching the quality of one's own dreams, as well as their independence from interpretation." The goal is the "invalidation of causal relationships."[23] Deleuze says something similar in his text on Beckett when he demands the suspension of reality. The point isn't to disavow facts and realities. The point is to strip them of their credibility and following. That has nothing to do with escapism or the starry-eyed denial of reality. The invalidation of reality opens the door to factual contingency. Müller and Deleuze approach Nietzsche's position when they conceive of their artistic and philosophical practice as an affirmation of contingency. Clinging to empirical facts is already the expression of a certain rigidity. It's the first step toward the obedience to authority that we call realism. The heightened realism of art and thought, in contrast, demonstrates itself in the enervation of the dominance of facts. New, unforeseen, or forbidden connections are forged. What is typically distinct and separate enters into volatile symbiosis—for

MARCUS STEINWEG

example, the mixing of seriousness and play. Without a playful element, all seriousness is risible authoritarianism. All play engages with coincidence. In playing, the subject is open to the instability of its reality and must confront its elementary impotence. Only by affirming the limits of its own capabilities does it create the possibility of a certain subjectivity. The subject experiences itself as an agent of its actions and decisions only in proportion to its own impossibility. On no account is the subject transparent to itself, nor does it possess a monadic selfhood. Ultimately, the subject answers for itself, without knowing itself. It is foreign to itself, but it doesn't evaporate away. Its self-reference is a form of play with its precarious identity in the space of facts and with all of the realities that continuously wash over it. There are causalities, legalities, probabilities, and rules, but nothing suggests that they are of the utmost inevitability. Nothing prevents us—in art as well as in thought—from playing with the most stable realities as with improbabilities.

SELF-TRANSCENDENCE

Badiou says that "Kant defines the human by means of something that exceeds humanity."[24] A proto-Nietzschean Kant, so to speak, recognizes in this excess the dynamic not just of thought, but of the subject in general. But in what way does the subject exceed itself? First it is necessary to consider the *a priori* character of excess. It is in no way an empirical transgression resulting from an act of will. What makes us pause to reflect in Kant is the subject's originary self-transcendence. The subject *is* in contact with its surroundings. Far from being an entity at rest within itself, it is elemental excess. Analogous to Heidegger's analyses of Descartes in *Being and Time* (1927)—in which the Cartesian question of how the cogito was reintroduced into the outside world after having been methodically separated from it was answered with the realization that it had always already been outside (as being-in-the-world)—Kant already claimed that the subject had long been outside. Something like the subject only exists as an outside subject. But isn't this outside, as a historical interpretation would suggest, simply history in the form of a sociopolitically codified space of facts? The outside that Kant had his subject border on is the noumenal sphere of the thing-in-itself. The noumenal limits the phenomenal (historic/historical) outer world by inscribing radical inconsistency into it. Broadly speaking, the difference between the phenomenal and the noumenal spheres is the difference between relative consistency and universal inconsistency. Accordingly, the subject's primordial self-transcendence indicates the subject's own level of inconsistency. Thus, Kantian reason can be considered a destabilizing factor within the subject economy. The subject is not reasonable because it limits itself to its capacity for understanding and does nothing that it cannot do. Rather, it is reasonable as a subject of constitutive self-overexertion catapulted beyond itself. That's why Badiou says, "The greatness of Kant is not at all to be found in his having proposed a theory of the

MARCUS STEINWEG

limits of reason, a theory of the human limits of reason. This aspect of Kant exists, but today it is devoid of any genuine force. The greatness of Kant is to have combined the idea of a limit of reason with its opposite, the idea of an excess of humanity with regard to itself, which is given in particular in the infinite character of practical reason."[25] This is so in the endlessness of practical reason, as in pure theoretical reason, which connects the subject to the impossible.

THOUGHT IN LOVE

You must remember that all thought is thought in love. It cycles through all of the hot and cold phases of feverish infatuation, its insecurities and hyperboles. This makes it a downright delirium. It gives it the dose of levity necessary to venture into the indefinite as into a nameless paradise. Paradisiacal thought? Certainly, as long as the condition of paradise confers an innocence on the subject that makes it nearly carefree. It's necessary to speak of the indifference at the heart of this experience. I'm in love when I'm prepared to lose sight of my goals in order to learn to see anew, which is the same thing as learning to see through the eyes of another. Love makes you blind, on the one hand. On the other hand, it sharpens your eye for the unseen and opens your thinking to the unthought. The subject slips into the dogmatic when its infatuation is lost to facts.

EYE

In Hebbel's diaries, we find the sentence: "The eye: an inward-facing minifying glass."[26]

NAIVETÉ

Naiveté is a critical condition. Just as you say that someone who has had an accident is in critical condition, you must also say it of the naive, though their lives may not hang in the balance. It means that the naive remain in a state of innocence in which they no longer belong. Children aren't naive. They move within the horizon of their skills and capabilities. He who believes he can ignore his knowledge and experiences is naive. Insistence on paradisiacal clue-lessness is inherent in naiveté. This makes it a narcissistic dilemma. Like someone in critical condition, the naive are suspended between two states, either of which they may enter. In their refusal to know what they know, their critical condition proves resistant to their critical capacities. There is no praise of naiveté that does not partake of it. You can celebrate the subject's carelessness and recklessness, its insanity and exuberance, as a condition of the possibility of its release from the shackles of affect. But naiveté doesn't have anything to do with astonished innocence. Naive are they who bottle up their innocence, who have long forgotten it.

BALANCE

Narcissism theory is fantasy theory that generates its own fantasies. The most common fantasy is that of the balanced subject: the idea that the narcissist suffers an irruption of the exterior or the real into his "interiority" as a destabilization that interrupts his "inner balance." The problem with this theory is that it fails to recognize the narcissistic subject's primordial fragmentation. It's not as if this subject were in balance. What we call the subject's balance is a fantasy construction that is a reaction to the experience of its ontological instability.[27] When Žižek draws on Freud and Lacan to write of the disturbance of the "narcissistic balance" by the stimulus of the real,[28] he perverts the actual problem of narcissistic subjectivity. The narcissistic balance indicates the subject's true state *ex negativo*: not one with itself, out of alignment with itself. The narcissistic self articulates the fissure that originally divided it, making it a sort of unhappy consciousness. If it were shown this fissure, which holds its self-image at a distance from objective reality in the symbolic order, it would be anything but surprised. The narcissistic subject watches over this fissure as if it were its most prized possession. The true narcissistic wound lies not in robbing it of its balance. The possibility of balance is far more injurious, as when someone—an analyst or therapist—tries to take its fragmentation away. The *noli me tangere* of the narcissistic personality means: no one may touch my fate to be unhappy forever!

GOD

God is a fantasy of excessive efficiency.

NIGHT

Descartes, Spinoza, and Hegel all agree in their various ways that substance becomes subject. In *Ego sum* (1979), Nancy demonstrated it for Descartes: "The radicalness, or originality if you prefer, of the Cartesian project is that it begins with chaos—inseparable and indistinguishable from chaos and from the subject. The basic precondition is at once the creation of chaos through a subject and the conception of the subject, which is generated through the material of chaos. The one requires the other. And so one must perforce assume that the *cogito*, the *thin* cogito itself, serves as a mask for something, which strictly speaking is neither soul nor god nor the world."[29] To see itself and to be itself, the subject must "transform the blindness of substance into vision."[30] It must communicate itself via the chaos that continues to pervade it. Thus, long before Deleuze and Guattari in *What Is Philosophy* (1991), Nancy could speak of philosophy, art, and science as the "chaoids" and define the cogito as "chaogito." Chaos and cogito have interfered with each other from the beginning, since chaotic substance yields to the fathomless foundation of the cogito-subject. As a result, the cogito remains immersed in the night of its substantial abyss. As an instance of a certain vigilance, it is marked by a sort of delirious light.

MARCUS STEINWEG

Instead of being transparent self-consciousness only for itself, it interrupts and unsettles the homogeneity of the nocturnal substance.[31] You could also say that by putting the substance of the eyes to use and making them see themselves, it inaugurates the drama of a self-inspection from which substantial being will never recover. The thing we moderns call the progression of Western philosophy adopts various contradictory approaches to interpret the tragedy of a self-illuminating night. We Westerners, you could say, have cast an unhappy eye on this night, on the darkness of a substance that does not exhaust or resolve itself in the subject. It will never manage to assign to it an ultimate cause, to place it on a *fundamentum inconcussum*—because this foundation, which Descartes sees in the cogito, is fragile from the very beginning. Admittedly, the cogito-subject can grant exile from the chaos or the night—that is effectively what it does; that is what we call thought—but it can't manage to represent it adequately, because successful adequation would tear it asunder. Everything would fall back into indifferent night, as if this light had never existed. What we call thought is the confrontation of one madness with another. In thought, the mute insignificance of substance intersects with the haywire light of cogitations that have lit out on their own path. Which is the greater madness can hardly be said. They have no common measure.

FACT WORSHIP

Those who invoke facts began to lose their foundation long ago. The reversion to facts has a precise function. It's supposed to make us believe that we are dealing in fixed realities. But facts are nothing more than facts. Only a heightened realism, emancipated from the religiosity of facts, can reclaim the concept for itself. Nietzsche recognized the most resilient strain of idealism in the belief in *petits faits*: "Seeing *what is*—that pertains to a different species of spirit, the *anti-artistic*, the prosaic."[32] Nietzsche does not say that artists have a connection to a deeper truth. To claim that would be a questionable romanticization of artists. He says that artistic production necessarily involves questioning all imperatives of fact, with which idealism (what we call realism) is supposed to be stabilized. If art is good for anything, it's the destabilization of all the fantasies that make the textures of our reality seem consistent. Art is the affirmation of reality's fragility and contingency.

SPLINTER

"The splinter in your eye is the best magnifying glass," writes Adorno in *Minima Moralia* (1951).[33] A sentence reminiscent of Lacan! And there is actually a sentence on psychoanalysis in the same section, section 29 in the book: "In psychoanalysis nothing is true except the exaggerations."[34] In his 1964 seminar *The Four Fundamental*

Concepts of Psychoanalysis, Lacan, who can seem like an exaggeration of Freud, associates the concept of the unconscious with what he calls his (psychoanalytical) "ontology." He refers to "the gap of the unconscious," whose main feature is its absence, as "pre-ontological."[35] Freud's theory of the unconscious culminates in Lacan's hyperbole of the real, which takes reality—the homogeneously woven fabric of facts, the symbolic order—to extremes, to the point where it begins to unravel and to communicate with its inexistence. Adorno's splinter takes on the function of the Lacanian real. It sharpens the eye for the invisible by directing it toward the inconsistent portions and not just the ocular evidence. The real is the best magnifying glass. It directs the gaze past the visible and on to the invisible. It trains the subject's ontological capacities by depriving the subject of its sight. Only blind eyes can see the nothingness in being. Only the blind see what remains dark in light. The actual object of psychoanalysis is what inscribes the dimension of objecthood and therefore the subject with inconsistency. This is why, as Serge Leclaire explains, its subject matter is the "unspeakable" (*l'innommable*),[36] to which Lacan assigns the term "the real." As unspeakable, the real marks a resistance in Lacan's topology, which is why its only synonym is the half-speakable truth that represents no object, but rather the unspeakable, monstrous thing (*chose*), which sticks like a bone in the craw of the speaking subject, or persists like a splinter in its eye. Persistence is generally a feature of reality that cannot be erased by avoiding or minimizing contact with it; in other words, whose existence cannot be touched by repression or negation. However, the existence of the real belongs to the order of inexistence, which is why the inexistence of god and therefore also the great other is exemplified in it as the symbolic order. Philosophy combines with psychoanalysis to communicate inexistence. Those who see only what is visible see almost nothing. Those who speak only what is speakable hardly say anything. The real allows the subject to come into contact with a boundary. You can call this contact *thought*, as long as you keep in mind that it's a thought that operates on the territory of immemorial forgetting.

ERROR PREVENTION

The logic of error prevention is neither the logic of thought nor the logic of art.

UNREAL

We don't call unreal that which falls outside the bounds of reality. The unreal is what falls *into* it, to become a part of it as an alien element. Unreality belongs to reality. It shocks or frightens the subject. Sometimes the unreal provokes the disorientation that we call thought. The merely real doesn't provoke thought. Only in the flash of reality's unreality does thought get underway. Suddenly the subject finds itself confronted with the puzzle of the world's existence. Wittgenstein called it a wonder.[37] But this wonder doesn't

MARCUS STEINWEG

attest to remote worlds. It bears witness to the remoteness of my world.

ELEGANCE

There is an elegance of thought that consists in its resistance to the imperatives of fashion at the very apex of the present. A mode of thought is elegant if it pierces the texture of the illusion called the present to reach the unknown. That is the painful tendency of elegance, its inherent melancholy or sadness. It disappears at the instant of its appearance. If it clings too long to the present, it is corrupted into mannerism. Inherent in thought is impotence in the face of everything that threatens to turn it into a style. Only when it is exposed or at least utterly defenseless can it free itself from the temptations of idiosyncrasy. Its elegance asserts itself in a here-and-now from which it distances itself by intensifying its contact with it.

HOLE

We think atop the foundation of indentitary certainties by drilling holes in it.

STINGING EYES

To look truth in the face—that is the cliché of thought because it can only do so in the face of a truth that remains faceless. "What thing," asks Nancy, "*can* be looked at directly in the face? If looking something 'in the face' means seeing its 'truth' or 'evidence,' then there is never any direct face-to-face. Every face is a bedazzlement, terrible and marvelous."[38] We know that Lacan calls the faceless face of the truth the real. Freud speaks of the unconscious, Heidegger of being that collapses into nothingness as nonbeing. There is no philosopher who hasn't found their own term for the truth without a face. Plato evokes the image of the shining sun. Burning light that stings the eyes. The sun inflames and irritates the subject. If it does not cause blindness, then at least it bedazzles. Like Freud's unconscious, Lacan's real, and Heidegger's being, it does not give of itself fully; it withdraws and withholds itself. It doesn't divulge itself directly. The subject communicates with these entities only at the cost of relative blindness. The truth generates a subject with stinging eyes. You can also refer to "reddened eyes," as Rancière does in a commentary on Deleuze.[39] With Deleuze, chaos blinds the subject and causes it to slide. What Deleuze and Guattari, together with Nietzsche, call chaos can be interpreted as a translation of the Lacanian real into the dispositive of immanent thought. The planes of immanence lie like a filter or a "screen"[40] over chaos. They muffle the contact with nothingness. Just as the antique logos already represented a neutralizing figure for the alogon, the immanence filter lies over the faceless chaos of truth in order to give it a face that stings the subject's eyes less. To look truth in the face means assenting to being blinded, which promises some minimum of insight. This perhaps impossible promise is the promise that philosophy makes to itself.

MARCUS STEINWEG

SUN

Thought follows a darkness that blinds the eyes as only the sun can: "Since the beginning of the Occident, it has been a question only of this; entering with eyes wide open into the night and/or into the sun itself,"[41] writes Nancy. There is a "clarity of obscurity" that repudiates the obscurantisms of the light as those of the darkness. Invisible light, impenetrable night. Invisible and impenetrable—and yet present, here and now. Deconstruction basically speaks incessantly of absent presence and present absence. You could also say that this clarity distances itself from the imperialism of comprehensibility. It generates a light that casts no shadows. It absorbs everything in darkness in order to transform it into stark brightness. The experience of night becomes the self-experience of thought, since thinking means turning to your boundaries like the inconsistency of meaning. By reaching into the night, the subject constitutes itself as the boundary of its world. In thought, it points toward the sun that collapses together with the night.

DICTATE

Roland Barthes explained in the late 1970s that "society" is supposedly "accused of forbidding desires, but I find that it mostly dictates them, imposes them, forces their satisfaction."[42] What he calls "society" corresponds with what Adorno understands under that concept in *Negative*

Dialectics, *Aesthetic Theory*, and elsewhere: the cultural, social, political, technical, and economically coded reality of facts, which *a priori* deny the subject "interiority" or "selfhood" or "authenticity" by conceding them only as fantasies and metaphysical projections. Nowhere is this more apparent than in the emotional economy, which encompasses sexual desires as well as romantic love and its organization into all of the varieties of "sexual liberation." Adorno also knew that the promise of freedom in the sexual realm is transmuted into a dictate at the moment it is instituted. And so it remains to this day: the imperative to *enjoy* robs passion, desire, and pleasure of an innocence they never had. Is nothing else left to the subject than to reconcile itself with the impossibility of innocence, with the irreducible presence of imperative dictates in the heart of love as in sexuality?

KAFKA

Who doesn't sometimes want to be alone, without any outside contact? Everyone has experienced the need for seclusion. In Kafka, it is "the desire for an unthinking, reckless solitude."[43] "I'll shut myself off from everyone to the point of insensibility. Make an enemy of everyone, speak to no one."[44]

EXILE

The subject after the death of the subject is exiled from itself. Driven out from its (supposed) core, it sees that

MARCUS STEINWEG

it has withered from itself. It is nothing other than this "insurmountable gap"[45] that marks Derrida's *différance*. In various and yet comparable ways, Levinas, Blanchot, Duras, Derrida, and Nancy began to measure this gap, in order to describe it as incommensurable. The subject is in exile because it only exists outside of itself.[46] Its exile status is no exception. It is normalcy.

IMPROVISATION

You can't not improvise, not when thinking, and not on any stage in the world. "I can no more improvise than escape improvisation,"[47] Derrida once said. That is the aporia of all thought: to be caught between two impossibilities, the impossibility of improvising and the impossibility of not doing it. Thought is stuck in this dilemma. Nothing else is left to it but to affirm this double impossibility as its situation. You can't not improvise because thought doesn't provide any last recourse. That's one version of the death of god: there is no such thing as the final argument, or what amounts to the same thing: the starting point, the first principle, the absolute origin. There is no mode of thought that is not in flux, which is not to say that it is necessarily arbitrary. To improvise means to assent to flux. Improvisation is the active affirmation of contingency. And yet, there is no thought that isn't instructed, channeled, contaminated, influenced, determined, and prepared. Thinking without a banister, as Hannah Arendt puts it, because every act of thought must make its way along countless banisters.

Before it even sets out, it is already situated in the wheel ruts not only of others' thoughts, but also of all possible conditions that pertain to the activity known as thought. This activity has been passivated from the outset, brought to a halt, steered. The impossibility of improvisation lies in this primordial orientation within preexisting spheres of meaning. The fact that god is dead doesn't mean that there is no meaning. It means that the one meaning is supplanted by an excess of meaning. There is an endless amount of meaning, and therefore there is none. There is no single, viable meaning. There is nothing but constructions of meaning, which pose countless banisters that the subject must make its way along in order not to plummet into the abyss presented by god's inexistence. Ultimately everything is nothing. Faced with this truth, which decimates every certainty, thought improvises without being able to count on the fact that it will work.

FEAR

When fear has gone, anxiety remains.

READING

Non-understanding is part of understanding. Because I don't understand, there is something to understand. There is no such thing as complete understanding, nor is there absolute non-understanding. To read a text—and in this case it's basically one and the same, whether it's a literary,

MARCUS STEINWEG

philosophical, or scientific text (boundaries that must be considered anything but firm)—is to experience this doubly: I can't avoid not understanding and I can't prevent myself from understanding (or at least understanding *something*). We shouldn't let ourselves be misled by rigorisms that claim there is nothing other than the opposition between understanding and not understanding. What does understanding mean in the first place? Must I empathize and recognize myself in the text I am reading? Is it part of understanding to have insight into the difference between the written, the described, the claimed, the recounted, and myself? Studying philosophical texts implies a constant questioning of the conditions and limits of understanding. The first issue is understanding the concept of understanding, to elucidate the history of its function and its use. This would require all languages. It would be an intractable task whose monstrosity communicates at least one thing to us: we don't have one unified concept of understanding. The challenge asserted in this word impels thought to hermeneutics, which must also be the *hermeneutics of hermeneutics*, the unrelenting questioning of the limits of understanding. Inherent in reading is the readers' excessive self-mediation with their own limits. When I read, I come into contact with the inconsistency of my evidence. In the act of reading, I constantly overstep my abilities. Either we read and affirm the dynamic known as reading as a questionable excess of our knowledge and abilities, or we simply do not read, which is to say that we immediately enter what we've read into the register of our own certainties.

BELIEF

As ever, a cold glance at the world warms the mind. We prefer to forgive god for not existing than to forgive Voltaire, Nietzsche, Sartre, Duras, Houellebecq, and others for proclaiming it. It's more comfortable to believe in a dead god than not to believe in one at all. The first lesson of Christianity: god is dead, now *believe* in him!

KITTLER WITH LACAN

Friedrich Kittler says that "consciousness is always on the outside,"[48] illustrating the compatibility of his theory of media with Lacan's psychoanalysis. Both are concerned with an ontology of exteriority in conflict with the metaphysics of interiority. On the psychoanalytic horizon, the fantasy of interiority is associated with the myth of a stable self-awareness. Psychoanalysis is the repudiation of such a self. Selfhood and individuality prove to be the cardinal illusions of the self's history of self-reference, a self that does not exist as such. That is why, with its concept of the real, Lacan's psychoanalysis establishes its conceptual correlate to Heidegger and Sartre's concept of nothingness. The fact that consciousness is outside means that it remains open to nothingness, which undermines all ontological consistency. Kittler's media studies are ignited by Heidegger and the early realization that "there aren't merely thoughts, but also words."[49] In that respect, it is already a theory of the signifier. You can't create meaning without

MARCUS STEINWEG

vehicles for meaning. The signifier determines the signified. It is its transcendental basis. Outside, the real—it isn't merely the future, that is, what will be and that which remains to be seen, as Derrida would put it. It marks the incommensurable core of all constructions of reality, be they political, cultural, social, religious, or aesthetic. *The real is what has already occurred. It is here and now.* How do we act toward it? I believe that the position known as realism above all serves the suppression or neutralization of the real (as the incommensurable). We flee into narratives that are no less idealistic because we call them realistic. Well, there is nothing beyond narration. Everything that we experience, think, and communicate is influenced by cultural dispositives and stereotypes. Ideology begins with the denial of this factual stereotyping. Ideological are those who deny being so.

SCRAPHEAP

First there is debris, unordered material, chaos. Heraclitus knew this: "The fairest universe is but a heap of rubbish piled up at random."[50] From this point on, the dialectic of order and chaos will dominate Western thought. It extends to Heidegger's "primal struggle" between "world" and "earth," in which the conflict between openness and closing or *aletheia* and *lethe* finds expression. Heiner Müller associates it with Foucault, by alleging that the ancient Greeks had a "measure" of the incommensurable, a knowledge of the irreducibility of chaos: "the cosmos as a scrapheap is still the most likely theory."[51]

HUMOR

What differentiates humor from irony and cynicism? The courage it requires! Irony is subtle destabilization of accepted evidence, cynicism reckless destabilization of the same. People who are ironic or cynical can be right without having to pay the price for it. Irony and cynicism contain self-exclusion from what they claim, while humor withholds all forms of protectionist self-exception. People who engage in critical dialectic have a sense of humor, because it recognizes no exterior, no solution or salvation—and it laughs about it!

HALLUCINATIONS

Hallucinating opens the subject's world to spirits. It opens a world within the world. All that it takes is for the door of consciousness to open minimally. Not to the familiar, which we call facts, but rather to the unfamiliarity of the familiar itself. Hallucinations are unreal realities. They haunt the subject like nervous ghosts. There's no reason to deny them entry to reality. They've already been here a long time.

SUBJECT

The subject is the placeholder and performer of chaos. Descartes already knew this, which is why he wasn't a Cartesian.

VISION

There is no totalitarian regime that isn't based on the fantasy of the all-knowing eye, as Christian monotheism is based on the doctrine of panoptical vision. Christianity is the religion of this eye; its god is an ocular authority. As long as we are seen, as long as someone is recording what we think, dream, and do—that is, as long as a conscience is at work in us, a daemon or a superego, ostensibly we aren't lost. The imperialism of light generates the dictatorship of transparency; the religious theater of sin presents a tragedy of light. The sun has lost its innocence. From this point on, the human subject seeks protection from it. This is why it flees into esotericism, obscurantisms, and extreme sports. We've known for a long time that god is dead, religion is a replacement for god, and esotericism in turn is a replacement for religion. Writing often approaches esotericism. Blanchot and Duras (and they're no exceptions) give it a sacral dimension—though insofar as it's possible, an areligious one. "To write," says Blanchot in the 1953 *La solitude essentielle*, "is to enter into the affirmation of the solitude in which fascination threatens. It is to surrender to the risk of time's absence. ... To write is to let fascination rule language. It is to stay in touch, through language, in language, with the absolute milieu ..., the opaque, empty opening onto that which is when there is no more world, when there is no world yet." At another point, Blanchot speaks of the experience of the "nothingness without consistency" that corresponds to this opening.

Always there is "contact at a distance," or immanent transcendence. It's a theme that gains importance with Derrida and Nancy, and which is also central to Deleuze's adoption of Nietzsche's category of the untimely. Nietzsche's project doesn't consist in the substitution of the fantasy of transcendence with an illusion of immanence, but rather in the atheist complication of the interlocking relationship between transcendence and immanence. That has nothing to do with a reversion to metaphysics or religion. On the contrary: it's an expression of awareness of the fact that insisting on pure immanence isn't any less metaphysical than the idealistic religiosity of transcendence. As always, things are more complicated than common sense would like to accept. Realism or immanentism produces its own religiosity. Transcendence in immanence doesn't designate some remote metaphysical world; in no way does it restore a positively conceived hereafter. "Rather," says Nancy in a text on Heidegger, "it must be understood as the thing that structures existence itself in the manner of the 'beyond' of ek-sistence." Analogous to Heidegger's denotation of the eksistence-character of being, transcendence means primordial openness to something that withdraws into the immanence of constituted reality. It's a transcendence that, as Roberto Esposito noted, "is not contrasted with but within, coinciding with immanence: *the subject's* excess."[52] Thus, the concept of transcendence does not adhere to any abnegation of the world or belief in the beyond. It simply limits religiosity in this world, which tries to place a pure here-and-now where the dead god used to be.

MARCUS STEINWEG

JAPAN?

Once when Foucault was asked about his interest in Japan, he replied: "Honestly, I am not constantly interested by Japan. What interests me is the Western history of rationality and its limit."[53] He also could have replied: You see, I'm not Roland Barthes. I distrust the supposedly symptomatic consistency of signs. Beyond semiology, I'm interested in the inconsistency or activities labeled natural, which wreck every system of signs. I'm interested in systems that aren't systems.

CATASTROPHE

The ancient Greek word *katastrophé* means "sudden change." In his interpretation of Plato's cave allegory, the word *katastrophé* may not appear, but Heidegger does speak of sudden change. It is the "essence of *paideia*."[54] We translate *paideia* as "education." But what does education have to do with catastrophe? The fact that education is catastrophic means first and foremost that it demands a change in the subject, who may remain a child (*pais*) no longer. In the Allegory of the Cave, this change contains a turning toward the real, that is, toward ideas. It presumes the turning of "one's gaze from the shadows."[55] Heidegger's pedagogy builds upon Plato to make it possible to differentiate the true from the untrue. Is it that easy? This same Heidegger, who based the "essence of 'education'" in the "essence of the 'truth'"[56] says of the truth (*aletheia*, "unhiddenness") that it reaches back to the *lethe* ("hidden-ness"): "The unhidden must be torn away from the hidden, in a certain sense it must be stolen from such."[57] However, at another point Heidegger also says that the "field of the *lethe* ... [denies] every revelation of what exists and there-fore also what is familiar. At the site of its essence, which it itself is, *lethe* causes everything to disappear."[58] We miss the point of Heidegger's pedagogy of catastrophe if we don't associate it with this disappearance. *Lethe* is like a black hole. It doesn't just absorb what exists; it also causes its appearance or unhiddenness to disappear. It erases the trace of the trace. That is the real catastrophe: the sudden change of what exists into nothingness. This change points to the "*Kehre im Ereignis*," the turn in the event, which Hei-degger associated with the counterturning of the truth. The term "counterturning" is key to Heidegger's 1942 lecture *Holderlin's Hymn "The Ister."* He points to the inherent ten-sion within be-ing (*Seyn*) itself, which collapses into the event, that is, with the concept that, as Agamben puts it, "designates both the centre and the extreme limit of Hei-degger's thought after *Sein und Zeit*."[59] Heidegger's thinking of the event proves to be catastrophic, because the event—which is to say the interlinked nature of *Sein* and *Dasein*, being and being-there—is itself catastrophic, inso-far as it keeps both poles distinct while at the same time keeping them in correlation. *Diaphora* is the Greek word for this difference, which posits the event as non-event, as the *withdrawal* and *absence* of its *complete essencing* (*Wesung*) = a rift in be-ing (*Seyn*).

MARCUS STEINWEG

HAPPINESS

François Jullien demonstrated that the idea of happiness was among the least questioned premises in Western thought. As long as this idea remains tied to a vision of a goal in order to inscribe itself in a teleology with a happy ending, it will belong to the Europeanism of the happy life, which "singled out the idea of happiness from the continuity of process and set it forth as 'the desirable' par excellence."[60] As always, Jullien approaches the deconstruction of one of the core categories of the European history of ideas from the outside, taking a detour through China, which did not undergo the separation of day-to-day living and the desire for happiness in order to nurture life independent of happiness. Nurturing life away from happiness means living it without any particular idea of happiness, beyond the dramaturgy of unfulfilled desire, without the romanticization of happiness. One thing that's notable about this comparison between European goal-orientedness/purposefulness and Chinese purposelessness/goallessness is that it leaves unmentioned the emergence of a conception of happiness within the field of Western philosophy that is freed from the categories of sense, from determination, and from telos. Nietzsche reactivated the antique and Spinozistic heritage of an immanence of *beatitudo* in the materialistic horizon of existence. Spinozistic/Nietzschean affirmationism, saying yes to life in its unliveableness, would be another strain of Western thought that locates happiness within its incommensurability—instead of

construing it as beyond life. Being happy simply means living. There is no life beyond life, beyond its violence and
unliveableness.

METRON

Nietzsche speaks of the "Aristotelianism of morals."[61]
He said it during and about his own era, and it still applies to
our own.

KNOTS

The question of the first cause is an archaeological question.
It is the foundation of the architecture of philosophy. Maybe
philosophy only exists in the form of concept architectures
poised over an origin (*arché*)—a first cause and foundation—
that doesn't exist. "How is it," Wittgenstein once asked, "that
philosophy is such a complicated structure?" After all, it
should be utterly simple, if it is that ultimate thing, independent of all experience, that it claims to be. Philosophy unravels knots in our thinking; hence, it must be simple, but its
activity is as complicated as the knots it unravels."[62] Philosophy is a complicated structure. Its result is simple, but
in action, it remains complicated. And yet the result
of philosophy cannot be separated from the activity of philosophy. In the *Tractatus*, you'll find the sentence: "Philosophy is not a theory but an activity." And: "Philosophy should
make clear and delimit sharply the thoughts which otherwise are, as it were, opaque and blurred."[63] There is only

MARCUS STEINWEG

philosophy as an activity whose results are constantly reassessed, which is not to say that it does not generate results. But its results are as inconsistent as the foundation they are built upon. *Arché* and *télos*, origin and goal, mark the inexistent past as well as the inexistent future of thought. Straining between two inexistences, thought moves across the porous ground of the present, which persists in its self-annulment.

MARKET

There is nothing beyond the market. Only idealism or moralism would argue with that. The market is everywhere, but that's why it isn't everything. Contradiction of the logic of the market belongs to the logic of the market. The market contradicts itself. That is the point of overlap between Hegelian speculation and the theology of finance. Both are able to function only under the condition of self-contradiction. The market runs riot in order to function. Philosophical speculation purchased its respectability on the bad checks of unsubstantiated concepts. Nietzsche spoke of the death of god. Lacan says that the big Other doesn't exist. Today we know that our realities dispense with backing in any final schema or from any ultimate bank. The speculative metaphysics of finance have inherited Christian ontotheology, in that they reconcile us to the emptiness of our realities.

BECKETT

The applause, recognition, admiration, or at least the attention that the activities of the circus performer elicit—earlier one might have said "commands"—exemplifies the narcissism of all subjects acting before a public, and of all who cannot but communicate their narcissism to this public through its denial or its exhibition (or in the best case, through the exhibition of denial). That is the truth of the stage and its immanent aporia. Feedback regarding events on the stage isn't just expected and encouraged; as something anticipated, it is inherent in the activities of the stage. No one sings, dances, makes music, writes, or speaks without expecting someone to take an interest. Even when we're alone, we remain on this stage, the theater of a subject that strives to compensate for its inconsistency through narcissistic projections, *imaginaria*. Is there a way out of this situation? Not as long as we connote it with an exterior. The only possibility to escape the narcissism of the stage is through humor, which inspires the mirth of staging aporia for the public as the uncrossable horizon of its existence. This is just what Samuel Beckett does.

GENIUS

Today if you read a text that, as so many do and with whatever warrant (there are thousands of reasons to do it!), takes up the genius aesthetic or believes to comment

on it critically, you can assume that it was written by someone who would never fall under the suspicion of being a
genius.

UNPRECEDENTED

We call something unprecedented that appears incomparable within the field of the comparable. A theory of exception
can only be a theory of incomparable comparability. It
marks the difference at the heart of identity, just as the
exception does the rule. Something that is completely
unusual wouldn't be exceptional and unprecedented, but
rather would be something that emphasizes its authority *ex
negativo* without completely assimilating it.

SELF-CONFINEMENT

There is no self-confinement that is not narcissistic. Narcissism is the narcissism of self-confinement. One thinks
of Walter Benjamin's *étui-man*. That's his word for the
velvet-lined box of consciousness. There are thousands of
other examples for this flight into the interior, for escapism
into an imaginary home or one's own presence. That's
always boring and reactionary. Above all, it's breathtakingly
stupid. You could write a cultural history of narcissism
that would coincide with a cultural history of stupidity—
which would also be a history of general cowardice and
regression. Of self-depoliticization with a clear conscience.
Of infantilism whose most basic activity consists in

interpreting everything new as a threat in order to indulge in political nostalgia, sentimentality, or narcissistic love of animals—we know what it means and how unselfless it is. "Anyone who likes cats or dogs is a fool,"[64] as Deleuze and Guattari write.

PAYING

In *Twilight of the Idols* (1888), Nietzsche writes: "The value of a thing sometimes lies not in what one attains with it, but in what one pays for it—what it costs us."[65] As we know, next to Hegel, Nietzsche is the representative reference for Georges Bataille's thought on sovereignty, which is characterized by measurelessness and heterogeneousness. Nietzsche's sentence expresses one of Bataille's premises: the opening of the economy onto the an-economic. In thought as in life, frugality is beside the point. They are irreversible wastes of energy. The subject doesn't just pay for its activities. Its costs reach into the incommensurable, in that it must pay more than it can pay. Those who truly pay are the ones who overreach their economic circumstances. In effect, this overreaching is what Bataille calls sovereignty. It implies excess. We could also call it placing excessive demands on the self. In that section of *Twilight of the Idols*, Nietzsche relates his "conception of freedom" to personal responsibility, or more precisely to "the will to self-responsibility": "For what is freedom? That one has the will to self-responsibility."[66] The price of freedom is the contestation of its existence. Since the subject is objectively unfree,

MARCUS STEINWEG

and freedom is not an option for it, it fights for it and in this way is able to attain a certain sovereignty. The same is true of truth—and here Heidegger's bypassing of truth and freedom in "On the Essence of Truth" (1930) comes to mind, which does not imply any agreement with him—it too is imaginable only at the price of recognizing its objective inexistence. Or, as Badiou put it: "The price of truth is breaking away from the self."[67] Only the subject that emerges from itself in order to leave itself in the undefined touches a truth that distances it from itself instead of forcing it to coincide with itself. To be a subject means to become a subject, someone other than oneself. Badiou was right to call Deleuze a model of a mode of thought that engendered itself, with Spinoza, with Nietzsche, with Blanchot (and therefore also, although Deleuze hardly wants to concede it, with Levinas), from an exterior (the "opaque power of the real"),[68] undermining its self-confinement and fantasies of interiority. That's what Nietzsche calls *paying*: to take upon oneself the costs of an incommensurable operation on oneself. Undoubtedly, this is a calculation that can only add up to failure.

BLINDERS

"Reality is more varied than enlightened thought can bear. Enlightenment can only exist with blinders. You can only take them off in art. Otherwise you're constantly in danger of running into something that doesn't fit the mold, and then you have to look away" (Heiner Müller).[69]

ENLIGHTENMENT

Should we call enlightenment the thing that spreads "trace elements of reason ... through the world," or is it "trace elements of chaos ... that bring forth enlightenment"? Alexander Kluge directs this question at Heiner Müller, who recognizes that it is the "purpose of intelligence" "to create chaos" in order to "question all illusions, all coalitions, and all alliances."[70] Ultimately, the point is to complicate the opposition between reason and chaos. What else does reason do than bring chaos into the world, and what does chaos produce if not the hyper-reasonable questioning of this chaos of reason, which is rationalistic totalism? The dialectic of enlightenment causes reason and chaos to interact in a way that does not privilege either side. We've gotten used to describing the birth of logos out of chaos or myth as the emancipation of thought from the irrational. At the same time, we know that the emergence of reason in the prerational sphere of chaos represented a violent event that generated chaotic effects. Translated into the system of nature/culture, that means that we distance ourselves from the myth of a culture that substitutes for "wild" nature, and cannot simply switch over to an opposing ideology of nature robbed of its "innocence" by culture. Nature isn't wild, pure, or innocent; nor is culture civilizing or violent. To formulate it as primitively as possible: one isn't better than the other. Nature isn't good, culture isn't bad; nor vice versa. Enlightenment begins with the suspension of these anthropomorphisms. Articulating oneself beyond good and evil is part of complexity. The interest-oriented, strategic, or irrational violence, brutality, and horror that happen in the name of (generally fascistic) naturalism and (ideological, religious) culturalism is the product of the subject's exit from the dialectic of enlightenment. Instead of acting at the level of its world's complexity, it reduces this complexity in favor of one-sidedness that it calls truth or justice. Should it make sense to speak of truth or justice in this context, then the dialectic of enlightenment teaches us that they are on the side of complexity rather than one-sidedness.

TWO KINDS OF OBSCURANTISM

In the section of *Aktive Passivität* (2014) entitled "The Aesthetic of Unknowing," Martin Seel follows Adorno's formulation of "determinate indeterminateness" in order to proclaim the "celebration of unknowing" as the "telos of all aesthetic perception."[71] He's undoubtedly right that uncertainty and unknowing are part of experiencing a work of art as well as aesthetic reflection. Adorno's formulation restricts the dimensions of the certain and the uncertain, the known and the unknown, the determinate and the indeterminate. Everything depends upon grasping the character of this restriction. You can speak of dialectic insofar as it remains a negative dialectic that denies itself a final synthesis. It's a dialectic of restlessness, in which the two corresponding poles abrade each other. The indeterminate is threatened by the determinate and vice versa. Initially, this mutual threat vitalizes both dimensions. They are what they are only through the contentious mediation of their opposite. This unrest is the measure of the progressive character belonging to this relationship of unrest, which also means that artistic thought and aesthetic reflection must escape these two forms of quietism: the obscurantism of unknowing, as well as the obscurantism of knowing. There is no complete knowing and no total unknowing. What we call art is resistance to this double obscurantism. Therefore, the expression "the celebration of unknowing" is misleading. Neither unknowing nor knowing is celebrated—if you can speak of celebration at all. It's this impossibility of privileging the one over the other, of making their relationship hierarchical, that is expressed in a work of art. The work of art is the theater of elementary resistance. If it celebrates anything, it's this impossibility. Art denies itself obscurantism, quietism, and dialectical synthesis. And therefore it also denies itself celebration and self-celebration. Art looks soberly on realities that elude its gaze. You can speak of a certain coldness of the gaze or of "controlled insanity."[72] The work of art constitutes the scene of the subject's self-transcendence. In it, reflection mingles with proflection, analysis with passion, intellect with affect, critique with affirmation. None of the poles leaves the others in peace. Only in their polemical intertwining and reciprocal irritation is there the possibility for art.

BREAK

The fact that every philosopher represents a break with the past, as Slavoj Žižek writes, does not relieve them of the necessity of also making a break with the future.[73] With the anticipated future that is robbed of its contingency, its *à venir*? Of course! But that's not all. Philosophy also breaks with the construction of a future without a past, precisely at the moment in which it wrests itself from it.

FLYING

Flying is a part of thinking. Kant knew that, but it caused him nothing but trouble. The *Critique of Pure Reason* (1781/87) declares a ban on flying by teaching reason to think or fly differently. The point is to think under the conditions of a subject that affirms its sensory nature. The subject must not fall back into precritical dogmatism. It experiences itself in its dependence on the forms of intuition of space and time. The one is dependence on its own receptivity, while the other is independence in the sense of hyperbolic or speculative openness to the indeterminate.

GOOD?

The good does not exist: the first rule of emancipatory politics!

SOUL

In a text on Paul de Man, Derrida says that the word *soul* "speaks to us at the same time of life and of death and makes us dream of immortality."[74] You could also say that by invoking mortality as well as the dream of immortality, speaking of the soul allows us to dream of an alternative to the system of mortality and immortality. Western thought sees the scandal of life that culminates in death as the horror of an immortality that anticipates eternal life as the true hell. T. S. Eliot placed a line from the *Satyricon* at the beginning of *The Waste Land* (1922): "Nam Sibyllam quidem Cumis ego ipse oculis meis vidi in ampulla pendere, et cum illi pueri dicerent: Σίβυλλα τί θέλεις; respondebat illa: ἀποθανεῖν θέλω." "I saw with my own eyes the Sibyl at Cumae hanging in a cage, and when the boys said to her: 'Sibyl, what do you want?' she answered: 'I want to die.'" Could the word *soul* be one that allows the living to dream of the certainty of their death as deliverance?

SPOILSPORT

Spoilsports aren't people who refuse to play. Spoilsports want to play without playing. They take away the critical factors: unpredictability and contingency. The thing that makes life difficult for them is that it itself is a game whose course remains indeterminate.

EMPTINESS

Emptiness marks a hole in the fabric of facts. It points to its fragility and contingency. Thus, it threatens determinism and all fantasies of closed causality. There is no thought that is not of emptiness, whatever name it goes under: nothingness or the abyss, the real or chaos, the incommensurable or contingency. Progressive thought moves toward emptiness instead of turning away from it by beginning to close the hole it represents with substitutes. The function of religion is, if not to interrupt contact with emptiness, then at least to minimize it. We're religious because god doesn't exist.[75] Religion is belief in god under the sign of his inexistence. Thinking implies the deconstruction of religiosity far more than the superior being called god, since the glory of god owes itself to his inexistence. We haven't yet learned to deduce god's ontological death from his factual inexistence.

OFFENDED

Pure illusion is always the illusion of purity.
—Martin Seel[76]

What Georges Bataille calls *sovereignty* resists the possibility of being offended. Sulking is no solution. To be sovereign is not to be invulnerable or immune to attack. You're sovereign if you resist the temptation of sulking when in actuality you are hurt. This requires pulling back from the logic of narcissistic offense-taking, which is associated with Nietzsche's *spirit of revenge*, with resentment and militant self-victimization. Psychoanalysis tells us that all realities that compromise my supposed self present a narcissistic offense-taking. You're offended if you arm yourself with a fantasy of integrity that is an idealistic construction. Why should the world orient itself around my fantasies? The real of reality consists in its indifference to everything imaginary. You could describe emancipation as pulling back from the logic of being offended, resisting illusions and projections that minimize our compatibility with reality, without assimilating to a fantasy of reality and a religiosity of facts whose function is to mitigate the heterogeneity, incommensurability, and inconsistency of the fiction known as reality.

TREE

"It is in no way necessary that the tree of science should have a single trunk," said Lacan in his seminar *The Four Fundamental Concepts of Psychoanalysis* (1964).[77] Couldn't we paraphrase this statement as such: it is in no way necessary that the tree of science should have a trunk at all. Would it even still be a tree? Yes, but one with treetops swaying over its roots.

MAD

Someone is mad if they're crazy enough to believe that they aren't.

STRUCTURAL HOMOLOGY

Why did Deleuze overlook the structural homology between his planes of immanence and Wittgenstein's language games and forms of life? Was it a mistake? Aren't both philosophers theoreticians of consistency, in that they intensify contact with inconsistency? Wittgenstein also gives space to (immanent) transcendence (of chaos or inconsistency) within immanence. Both develop, with and without Nietzsche, a mode of thought of privative transcendence. This connects them to Kant.

YES

Saying yes is more critical than saying no. Yes. No! Yes?

PRECARITY

To what degree can we depend on our language; how dependable is it? That is the question of language's consistency and the meaning that it generates. At the same time it is the question of the subject's ontological consistency, which Wittgenstein says is "a limit of the world." In the *Tractatus*, he says, "The subject does not belong to the world, but is a limit of the world."[78] That means that the subject does not unravel in the language community, which Wittgenstein later calls a *form of life*. It marks the limit of the logos community, since it continues to reference its inconsistency. The decisive factor is that what is beyond the limit collapses into the limit itself. It's not a simple outside or a positive elsewhere. It's an implicit beyond, an intrinsic exterior whose limit the subject marks *qua* subject. The *Tractatus*'s famed seventh proposition—"Whereof one cannot speak, thereof one must be silent"[79]—allows language to touch this outside, which attests to more than the silencing of language in the environs of the *mystical* that only *shows* itself but does not allow itself to be *spoken*. In his 1930 *Lecture on Ethics*, Wittgenstein associates the dimension of the mystical with the category of wonder. How do you describe the "experience of wondering at the existence of the world"?[80] Apparently not in the mode of "significant language,"[81] not in the mode of meaning and sense, not in the mode of the sentence or the preposition. At the same time, the desire to progress beyond the "limits of language," this "running against the walls of our cage," though it may be the "tendency of all men," is "perfectly, absolutely hopeless."[82] That is exactly the problem. The problem of language—language as a problem—has to do with this conflict, which the first sentence of the preface to the first edition of the *Critique of Pure Reason* (1781) already described: "Human reason has the peculiar fate in one species of its cognitions that it is burdened with questions which it cannot dismiss, since they are given to it as problems by the nature of reason itself, but which it also cannot answer, since they transcend every capacity of human reason."[83] Apparently it is proper to the nature of reason— to the *essence* of the subject, if you can momentarily accept this essentialism as part of the problem at stake here—

MARCUS STEINWEG

to refer to the limit of its abilities.[84] Humans have the tendency to want to progress beyond this limit, outside the cage of their reason, their language, their world. This is the core of the problem and the problematics that Kant proposed. "I call a concept problematic," writes Kant, "that contains no contradiction but that is also, as a boundary for given concepts, connected to other cognitions, the objective reality of which can in no way be cognized." He continues, "we have an understanding that extends farther than sensibility problematically," beyond the "sphere of objects." Kant's example of this kind of problematic concept is of course "the concept of a noumenon," which is "merely a boundary concept" whose function is to "limit the pretension of sensibility."[85] An originary self-transcendence belongs to the Kantian subject, which is to say the self-extension of reason beyond the phenomenal sphere; however, this beyond collapses into the limit that differentiates it from the phenomenal. This collapse of the limit and what is beyond it marks the concept of the problematic. This also means that the noumenal space is indistinguishable from this limit. The problematic confronts thought with the puzzle of the indistinguishable. It would be problematic to call the unspeakable the uncircumventable "background," as this background can exist only as an abyss. Instead of being load-bearing ground, the background of the unspeakable is what the experience of speech—speaking in (logical) *propositions*—holds open against abyss of the inexpressible. Wittgenstein's accomplishment lies in the fact that he did not seal the abyss of the inexpressible, recognizing its problematic *function* for the logical propositions. The problematic is a concept that points to the nonphenomenal—that is, the noumenal—reverse side of the world, of reason, of language, toward what with Wittgenstein we can call the dimension of the mystical, but also of the ethical and aesthetic. The problem of language is therefore a problem first because it indicates that it is constantly used illegitimately, in the attempt to go beyond language by means of language. Second, it is a problem because language borders in a positive way, if you can put it that way, on the sphere of the extralingual (the unsayable and the unthinkable), and therefore also on its own inconsistency and unreliability. The problem of language and the question of what you can rely on coincide in the dilemma that you must rely on something that you cannot rely on. We must rely on our forms of life and language games, says the late Wittgenstein. We must *accept* them like the ground we walk upon.[86] But that doesn't mean that we have ground to rely on, final ground, final certainty, since every form of life and every language game remains contingent, a sort of floating architecture erected on a foundation that is in no way stable. When we say *ground*, we imply a certain reliability and consistency. Ground that wasn't at all consistent would be no ground at all. However fragile the ground may be, it is only ground when it provides a minimum of support. The ground that supports the body of thought (of questioning, skepticism, or doubt) must be safe to walk on. As we know, in his *Meditations on First Philosophy* (1641) Descartes planted this ground under philosophy, a *fundamentum certum et inconcussum*, a certain and unshakable foundation that is the *ego cogito*, the *I think*, the thinking I. Since its beginnings, philosophy has articulated itself as an investigation into the consistency of its own conditions, by seeking *archaí*, first causes, that is, principles that can provide such ground. It seeks the origins of reality. Reality is what I call the world as it appears or is, the constituted space of facts. Facts have the function of suggesting reliability and solidity. When we speak of the realities of facts, we're speaking of things that are marked by a certain permanence and solidity, even if they remain precarious. Maybe philosophy is nothing more than the willingness to open oneself to this precariousness, which basically means accepting that the ground is porous.

TREMENDOUS

The Ancient Greek word *deinós*—which owes its power to its central position in the first stasimon of Sophocles's *Antigone*, as well as the weight that it received via Hölderlin's translation in the thought of Heidegger, Derrida, and Lacoue-Labarthes—can be translated as *tremendous*, instead of the typical *frightening*, *monstrous*, *woeful*, and the like. The tremendous falls outside of the normal and marks its limits. Something that is tremendous distracts us with its conspicuousness. The subject is easily thrown off balance when confronted with the tremendous, until it finally understands itself as tremendous, as the monstrous exception to the context known as nature in its supposedly cosmic balance, and, in the secular continuation of medieval conceptions of order, to regularity.[87] The collision of man and nature corresponds to the conflict between two enormities. The hubris of reason freeing itself from natural order has its equivalent in nature, which is indifferent to it. François Châtelet described the project of "the invention of rationality" as a hyperbolic adventure whose audacity can hardly be contested. The "tremendous responsibility"[88] that philosophy saddles itself with is an expression of childish irresponsibility. Philosophers are children who declare that their games are reasonable. They have good cause to do so, but no ultimate cause. Heraclitus already said this in fragment 52 (*αἰὼν παῖς ἐστι παίζων, πεσσεύων· παιδὸς ἡ βασιληίη*: "Eternity is a child playing drafts, the kingly power is a child's") by declaring a child to be the archon in the game that is the world. Its responsibility correlates to excessive irresponsibility. That lends it a carelessness that Greek thought would label *deinós*: massive, troubling, tremendous.

HEGEL

Hegel is an (anticipated) reaction to Nietzsche, although everyone thinks it's the other way around.

TASTE

Should we detect elitism of perception and judgment when Nietzsche speaks of "*small* taste" in reference to Robert Schumann, which he associates with "a dangerous propensity, doubly dangerous among Germans, for quiet lyricism and sottishness of feeling": "constantly walking off to withdraw shyly and retire, a noble tender-heart who wallowed in all sorts of anonymous bliss and woe, a kind of girl and *noli me tangere* from the start"?[89] Or on the contrary, isn't Nietzsche speaking against elitist sensitivity and the narcissism of the beautiful soul that arms itself with its tenderness to deny contact with realities with which in truth it has long been reacting to? Marcel Duchamp banished taste from art because it exists only as small taste, as narcissistic defensiveness and romantic self-celebration, a posture that avoids contact with the tasteless real by excluding it from its image of itself and the world. Taste is intrinsically autoerotic and reactionary. This is why Nietzsche can say that unlike Beethoven and Mozart, with Schumann "German music was threatened by its greatest danger; losing *the voice for the soul of Europe* and descending into mere fatherlandishness." The romanticism of small feeling and fragile sensitivity mark an exit from the sphere of emancipatory politics.

POLIT-HYSTERIA

Postpolitical quietism gave way some time ago to polit-hysteria. The allocation of guilt with a clear conscience has taken the place of analysis. The political, recently absorbed by politics, is now neutralized by pseudopolitical moralism. Self-depoliticization through overpoliticization: if everything is political, nothing is political anymore. To be on the left today must mean winning back the political,[90] and resistance against quietist as well as hysterical reaction.

TEARS

Public crying, whether out of distress, relief, or despair, is a political reality today. The exhibition of empathy and feelings is the dictate of a society that is increasingly depoliticized, in that it stages politics as a drama of conscience and a comedy of justice. The dictatorship of tears now holds sway over all areas of public life. Reality TV, including its quasi-theological confession culture, which demands the empathy-stimulating dissemination of what its protagonists call their story or their life, motivates the mobilization of emotions that are brands of active nonthought. Videos on the Internet of singing children pushed into the limelight by their parents, of tears of emotion from a protesting flash mob, cute kittens, or elephants reunited after decades of separation are supposed to activate "feelings." Never has the desire to be overwhelmed to the point of speechlessness been more widespread than today. To finally be allowed to cry, defenseless against your own emotions (or what you consider them to be), to have an image offered up to you, to give your feelings free rein—this is part of the prevailing regressive mood of "emotional capitalism" (Eva Illouz). This collective emotional kitsch is the precise complement to neoliberal efficiency of thought—a symptom and result of general depoliticization. The narcissism of cold-heartedness articulates itself as a religion of feeling.

MARCUS STEINWEG

ETERNAL CHILD

Behavior that belongs to the normalcy of interpellative self-constitution in children continues in adults as regressive narcissism: constant clamoring for attention and confirmation, theatrical self-centeredness, rigorous instrumentalization of others, difficulty making decisions, libidinal rejection of reality, autocracy, sensitivity, self-righteous celebration of one's own feelings, melodramatic body esotericism, self-objectification, the pathos of innocence, extortionate lachrymosity.—All of this is the desperate wish to eternally remain a child!

DREAMING

Who would deny that in every dream, whether it's abstruse, obscure, evident, or confusing, instead of a truth another dream is concealed whose meaning consists of the annihilation of meaning? That would be the dream-born dream of a reality beyond dreaming.

VANISHING POINT

Thought's vanishing point isn't located in what exists. Thinking means breaking rank with what exists—not in order to indulge in the imaginary. To withdraw from the existing is to exit the fiction known as reality. Does that mean that there are no realities? It means that the things we refer to as such lack any validity. Thinking implies the experience of the world's invalidity. The cosmos is incommensurable. It doesn't have any value. Not closing one's mind to cosmic indifference is part of the basic experience of philosophy.

PUTTING WORDS IN SPINOZA'S MOUTH

I don't deny that god is almighty, I contest his existence!

PERSISTENCE

A system is complex if it stands at odds with the totality of its elements. Complex realities characterize an excess of reality that Nietzsche calls chaos, Adorno non-identity, and Lacan the real. What, then, would be a mode of thought that is commensurate with complexity, or, what would be a mode of thought of the complexity of our world? It would be thought that turns to face the unthinkable by beginning to think through this surplus. When Plato located the idea of the good (*idea tou agathou*) beyond being (*epekeina tes ousias*), he defined philosophy as a confrontation with the nothingness in being, which returns later in Heidegger's formulation of being as nothingness. Does that make Plato the thinker of transcendence and dual-world ontotheology? Yes, but only insofar as he is also a thinker of immanence, in that he bars the highest idea from the reality of being constituted by simple ideas and their manifestations. In this act of separation, Platonic thought presents itself as immanence-based thought, which recognizes immanent transcendence in the sun that is barred from being. The

MARCUS STEINWEG

idea of the good, the all-illuminating sun, itself remains unseeable, and is barred from the constituted order as the dark or black or inscrutable basis of being. It is the excess that negative dialectics formalize as the remainder that cannot be incorporated into dialectic. Essentially, this remainder collapses into nothingness or god, assuming that what we refer to here as nothingness or god doesn't exist, without therefore being inefficient. In the psychoanalytical register, it is the unconscious, which persists in obstinate latency.

FRENZY

Thought can express itself as delirium and frenzy. It engages in a motion that leads the subject out of itself to new things. As part of its unsecured nature, it risks experimentation whose course and results remain uncertain. The subject drills a hole in its present situation. It slips through it without knowing where it is headed. This is why—because of this nearly reckless motion—it must proceed as precisely as possible. There is no contradiction whatsoever between frenzy and precision. On the contrary, they necessitate each other. If you are closed to all frenzy, you aren't thinking. Openness to unknowing is part of thought. Thinking means being crazy in a precise way.

ROMANTICISM

You can call *romanticism* the desire for desire, as it so often occurs. There is another, hardly less narcissistic romanticism. Instead of departing from the beloved other by leaving them behind in order to have the license founder passionately on the distance between you, the subject of this second romanticism approaches its object with mild indifference. *I love and desire you—which means my love and desire apply to you and therefore have nothing to do with me!*

LANGUAGE

Someone is a subject if they put up resistance to language, make it falter or stumble. It is language itself that the subject antagonizes. No subject finds a way to connect with itself through language. At best, it manages to discover its own inconsistency by means of language. That is what you might call writing: the identification of inconsistency in language, which is the deceptive zone of familiarity and the elementary space of the uncanny. When Žižek says you have to "think in language, but against language,"[91] it implies the necessity of thinking against the illusion of familiarity as well as the romance of the uncanny. That only works in the murky waters of language if the subject moves itself, sometimes by swimming and sometimes by floating along. Thinking means—instead of giving in to the fantasy that there's a simple space beyond language and you could step out of it as you could out of a polluted river—mixing more poison into it, in order to increase its degree of toxicity to the limit of what can be survived.

MARCUS STEINWEG

THIEF

What does the thief want? What is his desire directed at? At the thing he takes, you would say. But what is the thief stealing by taking something that doesn't belong to him? We have to discern between the object of the theft and the object of his desire. The thief never desires the object that he steals! It acts as a substitute for the thing he desires. The goal is to possess the unpossessable. In Lacan it is called the *Real* or the *Thing*. In his seminar entitled *The Ethics of Psychoanalysis* (1959–60), he differentiates between the object of desire and the Thing as object-cause of desire, with the Thing as the limit of the object system, which is to say constituted reality or symbolic order. It is the hole in the object and marks the vanishing point of the ontological system.[92] Every desire refers to this point, as long as desire means turning toward the limit of the positive order of being. Another name for this order would be the world of laws, rules, and possibilities—the system of facts. To desire is to cast doubt on the legitimacy and plausibility of this system. How does the thing that is desired differ from the object of theft, then? That you can't possess it, or that it can only be possessed by stealing objects in its place! You steal to possess the unpossessable. Stealing is a romantic act.

HORROR

Horror is the fright that causes the subject first to tremble, then to freeze. Faced with the inconceivable, its coordinates and concepts fail. Horror provokes a loss of language that can lead to madness. It opens a passage in the middle of the world that leads not to another world, but to this one in its factual indifference. By means of sense, horror shreds the promise of sense in the coherence known as the world. It reveals the naked incoherence of the world.

GUTTER

The truth lies in the gutter. That's according to the religion of authenticity that presents itself as the wisdom of the gutter. At least people who come from the gutter haven't just stumbled into reality out of the university, parliament, a church, or some other cloud of fog. The gutter is the school of life that believes itself to be untouched by all of that. It's just that the gods were driven out of the gutter long ago. There are other idols roaming about—idols whose "false immediacy" is worshiped, as Adorno and Horkheimer put it. "Street cred" is just another name for it. The world would be so simple if there were beautiful gutter souls who owed their purity to the experience of impurity. It's not just that the gods live in the gutter; the gutter is present in every castle and cathedral. If you were to try to explain the global success of the religion known as capitalism, you could say its secret lies in the fact that it came from the gutter.

A MINUTE TOO MANY

The note titled "Reprise" from Paul Valéry's 1941 book *Tel quel* comes to a nearly proto-Lacanian conclusion: "Il y a dans toutes les existences, une minute de trop que l'on paierait infiniment cher pour reprendre à la réalité.—Alors ce réel *qui est de trop*, devient cauchemar. In every existence there is a minute too many, for which one would pay infinitely dearly to take back from reality.—And so this reality *that is too much* becomes a nightmare."[93] Actually the minute too many marks the real as the incommensurable excess of reality. It is the moment that cannot be integrated, which strains the homogeneity of my construction of reality and threatens to tear it apart, the hole in being or the immanent outside, the tear in the texture of facts. This infinitesimal quantum is exorbitant for every subject. In truth, it's this minute too many that explodes the continuum of time. It is the interruption of causality and linearity, and thus indicates the impossible self-coincidence of every subject. In this way, *the surplus reality in the midst of reality*, which Lacan calls the real, the point of inconsistency in my reality, becomes a nightmare. Here is where the finite and infinite intersect. Essentially, the intrusion of the infinite into my finiteness becomes perceptible in the experience of the minute too many. The infinite intrudes on my order as chaos. It reveals it as illusory. The finite is already infinite, just as the real is the truth of reality and heterogeneity is the truth of the homogeneous. We experience things as nightmares that shake our fixed certainties to confront us with their fragility. My nightmare differs from a "normal" dream in that it breaks with my normalities. In it, the subject comes into contact with its truth, which is its openness to the infinite—not only in the theological-religious sense of the word, but rather in the sense of an infinite minute or an isolated intensity and eternity.

JOURNEY

Human beings move from nothingness to nothingness. That's the journey you can call life. We're under no obligation to interpret it as a tragedy and stage it as a drama. What's more reassuring than the certainty of an end? The child might shy away from sleep each evening. But before it falls asleep and fatigue descends to close its eyes, it experiences the gentle loss of self between waking and sleep. Not yet asleep, but no longer awake. If there is a paradise—and there are a thousand reasons to think so—it is related to this intermediary reality. Awake, the subject experiences nothing but trivia. Asleep, it dreams up a heightened vividness that shuns the light of day and resembles exaggerated comicality. Only in the middle of this state of affairs between day and night does it set out on a journey that can be endless. In this way for a moment it resists its obliteration.

LOVE

We don't love for no reason, as romantic convention would have it. And yet, everyone knows that loving for good reason makes love impossible. Neither love-pragmatism nor the narcissistic self-abandon we call altruism lays a finger on the wonder between eros and agape, immanence and transcendence. Deleuze accuses Richard Wagner of being "too infatuated with transcendence"[94] (an accusation that Mehdi Belhaj Kacem repeats in reference to Badiou[95]), only to recognize an immanent mode of thought in Verdi, while at an Italian opera with François Châtelet. It's a mode of thought that resists not just transcendence, but also all of the calculations of immanence that can manage without wonder. The "dance of the resounding molecules"[96] belongs to music as to love. In it, the back-and-forth motion between lovers resounds, which is irreducible to either. Without any apparent connection, molecules jump from here to there and back. Love can be just as absurd and logical, contingent and necessary. It's a mathematics of asymmetrical ardors gone haywire. The carnival of emotions opens the space between immanence and transcendence. It neither bows to the authority of the vertical nor the no less imperious dictatorship of the horizon. To love is to generate resistance to horizon and origin. Lovers live in the interstice of space and time. They have their reasons and they know them well. But they don't have any reason to trust their reasons! The wonder they partake in draws an asymptotic line. Like music, love is "humanity's most rational activity."[97] It opens itself to meaning that is as immanent as it is infinite.

CATHOLIC

A Catholic is someone who renounces the pleasure of renunciation.

ASH

Maurice Blanchot and Jacques Derrida aren't the only ones who have meditated on the relationship between script, writing, words, and ash, fire, the disaster between being and nothingness, and inferno or holocaust, although they knew that what they'd written hardly provided more than the trace of its inconsistency, already at the moment of its writing.[98] The trace retroactively takes the place of what was. It attests to an originary absence. This original vacancy has thousands of names. You could define philosophy as the unending attempt to give it yet another precisely because the thing in question is nameless, the hole in the nomenclature, of which Badiou, with Lacan, has said that it marks, as the real, the "impasse of formalization,"[99] or of thought. This impasse, this spot of nothing, this impossibility that nonetheless supports everything—all political hopes, amorous fantasies, and economic promises—indicates the ontological inconsistency of all ontic-empirical consistency, which, in order to be, must place its trust in that which is not. We know that Pier Paolo Pasolini composed a poem entitled "Le ceneri di Gramsci" ("Gramsci's Ashes"). Badiou comments on this text in *À la recherche du réel perdu* (2015). For him, Pasolini is a thinker "of great power" and "infinite appetite," and to an even greater degree in his poetry than in his prose and films, he is "very close to the point of impossibility."[100] He lingers there. He moves there. He reinvents himself there—like every thinker who isn't settled in the possible or the existing! To think is to remain focused on the impossible, on the reality of the destruction of reality that is indicated by the real. That makes it a nearly reckless act, which entails the willingness to start all over again from the beginning, to bet everything on a single card, and therefore must be blind, bordering on fanaticism. Every attempt to rethink and reconfigure the world and the milieu in which I live and to which I belong carries within it the seed of destruction, a sort of poetic violence. Walter Benjamin wrote about the destructive character that came to represent artistic activity to him. Creation and destruction are in league with each other. Derrida's deconstruction, which proceeds from Heidegger's destruction, tells us the same. And Catherine Malabou's concept of plasticity fuses both dimensions. There is no stable exit from the logic of destabilization because destabilization belongs to the (re)production of the new. The heart of the new already contains its own ashes. Deleuze spoke of exhaustion and decline. And Foucault doesn't have any illusions about it either: "So, out of all those illusions, what do we have left? Well, we have the ashes of a handful of words."[101]

BRILLIANT

People call lectures brilliant when they understand them!

IDOLS

In *Twilight of the Idols*, Nietzsche defined philosophy as destruction, which found an echo in Benjamin's *destructive character*, as in Heidegger's *destruction* and Derrida's *deconstruction* of metaphysics. By destroying idols, philosophy refutes the evidence of its era. It does not demonstrate its inexistence; it demonstrates its inconsistency and contingency. In doing so, it disassembles the dispositive, in which these certainties are organized as stable factors. Nietzsche spoke of the "campaign against *morality*,"[102] where morality is not limited to morals, but implies all structures, patterns, and intellectual cultures that dominate our relationship to the world and our understanding of truth: "That which is called *idol* on the title page is quite simply that which has hitherto been called the truth. *Twilight of the Idols*—in plain terms: the old truth is coming to an end ..."[103] This coming to an end is nothing external to truth. Truth contains its untruth, as it is constantly aging. The old truth stretches to the new one, which will become the next old one. Truth proves to be an idol as long as you fail to recognize the dynamic of its transformation, which is its self-deconstruction. "All that philosophy can do," writes Wittgenstein, "is destroy idols. And that means not making any new ones—say out of 'the absence of idols.'"[104] If what Wittgenstein means here isn't just that idols shouldn't be replaced with other idols, but that philosophy must not replace the destroyed idols with the idol of the absence of idols, then his claim can be theologically and ontologically interpreted as such: it's not enough to replace one truth with another. Everything depends upon learning to abstain from truth by beginning to abstain from abstaining from truth.

MARCUS STEINWEG

COMPLICATED

To be clear to the same degree to which my life is complicated. Or, as Foucault puts it: "I do not like obscurity because I consider it a form of despotism."[105]

EXHALE

Apologists of becoming, of transformation, of the break with what exists, of change, are accused of giving in to illusions that have long since been refuted by a capitalism that presents itself as flexible and creative. Don't they understand that all concepts can be misused and must come under suspicion without lapsing into invalidity for that reason? Don't they understand that thinking means operating with problematic parameters, with materials that are as toxic as they are recyclable? They don't understand because they've never entered into a mode of thought that, instead of being promising, hygienic, opportunistic, and integral, drives the subject into a dynamic of self-transcendence, rather than letting it exhale in self-satisfaction with the clear conscience of active nonthought, which believes in a kind of "thought" beyond the existing (beyond history and its contamination),[106] thus proving itself idealistic even as it considers itself critical.

HEIDEGGER

Should we still read Heidegger after the publication of *The Black Notebooks*, with the knowledge of their anti-Semitic content? Absolutely! Reading an author does not mean agreeing with him or her. Reading means taking on the risk of tantalizing uncertainty. If you only read what you like, you've hardly begun to read. In reading, the experience of hyperbolic overload manifests itself. Those who read experience the inconsistency of their world.

PRECISION

A nearly imperceptible line divides precision from fastidiousness. Maybe precision can exist only—in writing, science, art, politics, and love—under the threat of becoming fastidiousness. Precision makes exact cuts. It proceeds meticulously, not slowly. Those who are precise can do so at high speeds. They almost have to, in order to make clean cuts. You could say that the condition for precision is that it operates at high speed. Those who are fastidious proclaim slowness as the law of precision, and hold to it. Fastidiousness submits to the dictate of the correct. It decelerates all of the subject's processes, subjecting it to the fear of insufficient precision. Thus, it lapses into punctiliousness and pedantry. Driven by fear to the limit of its capacity to act, the fastidious subject is a passive, narcissistic subject. Precision, on the other hand, demands being carefree at some minimum level, as an affirmation of contingency. Together with Mallarmé, Kafka represents precision in the face of universal coincidence. This makes them absolute poets: that they manage to unite precision and contingency.

FANATICISM

Nothing causes the subject to become more fanatical than a mode of thought that denies its excesses.

UNRECONCILED

The claim that "the work of art ... loses all value" when the artist "in any way attempts to insinuate a reconciliation with the human situation and world condition" comes from Friedrich Hebbel.[107] Though irreconcilability is part of the work of art, that doesn't mean that it exhausts itself in negativity, the pathos of the critical, or in wounded defensiveness. Distancing yourself from resentment and victimization is part of art. Its approach is characterized by assertiveness and confident affirmation of the incommensurable. Completely immersed in world affairs, fully confronting the aporia of human existence, the work of art is the arena of controversial humor. In all significant works of art, laughter at the futility of our constructions of meaning triumphs, at the critical remorse of those who style themselves victims of their realities. This is why Adorno could imagine the compossibility of the reconcilable and irreconcilable. Dialectic can only begin with the interweaving of these two terms. Like Hebbel, Adorno doesn't consider pursuing a dialectic of reconciliation that (right or wrong) is associated with Hegel's absolute idealism and whose function lies in a reactionary arrangement with developments in the world: "The reconciled condition would not be the philosophical imperialism of annexing the alien. Instead, its happiness would lie in the fact that the alien, in the proximity it is granted, remains what is distant and different, beyond the heterogeneous and beyond that which is one's own."[108] The irreconcilable reconciliation that Adorno—and Hebbel, in his way—suggests is the affirmation of the distant and the various as an incommensurable measure, in that they cannot be identified, marking the truth of our world as nonidentical.

RESURRECTION

The continual resurrection of divine imperial power and authority, of god's omnipresence, is the apodictic proof of his inexistence.

PRISON

Just as you can speak of the body as the prison of the soul and the soul as the prison of the body, you can also speak of imagination as the prison of the subject. It's not the thing that opposes social, political, and economic imperatives. Society, politics, and the economy are imaginary systems who owe their consistency to their inhabitants' powers of imagination. The glue of these systems consists of social, political, and economic fantasies. Only breaking with them reveals the inconsistency of their contents. Only in breaking with reality does the subject come to understand its fantastic character. Breaking out of the prison of the imagination means breaking with insinuated realities. "There is nothing outside of prison," says the philosophical doxa. "Yes there

MARCUS STEINWEG

is," answers the escapee. "Prison may be everywhere, but therefore it isn't everything!" "So what awaits you beyond its walls?" "Former prisoners pleading to be let in!"

NAKED

Imagine a human who is completely unattached to their past and present, who views their own life with the utmost apathy, as detached as if they were viewing someone else's, and who at the same time experiences the greatest happiness, a happiness that is like a contentment unrelated to satisfaction, but rather due to indifference, to deep equanimity, sheltered from all expectations and disappointments, freed from the usual effects that prevail over our inner lives, a human who has shed their self in order to take on another form of existence, similar to that of a stone or a cloud, someone who is willing to be little more than no one, the faceless witness to events that form it. Would this human beyond humanness be the pure form of humanity?

PUTTING WORDS IN NIETZSCHE'S MOUTH

I fear nothing, I'm afraid!

SUGGESTION

Kafka's story entitled "At Night" is well known:

Deeply lost in the night. Just as one sometimes lowers one's head to reflect, thus to be utterly lost in the night. All around people are asleep. It's just play acting, an innocent self-deception, that they sleep in houses, in safe beds, under a safe roof, stretched out or curled up on mattresses, in sheets, under blankets; in reality they have flocked together as they had once upon a time and again later in a deserted region, a camp in the open, a countless number of men, an army, a people, under a cold sky on cold earth, collapsed where once they had stood, forehead pressed on the arm, face to the ground, breathing quietly. And you are watching, are one of the watchmen, you find the next one by brandishing a burning stick from the brushwood pile beside you. Why are you watching? Someone must watch, it is said. Someone must be there.[109]

Whether it's a parable or a story, Kafka's text touches on the inconsistency of human existence. The word "safe" suggests a consistent relationship to the world, not once but twice ("in safe beds, under a safe roof"), how the people sleeping all around are like a fallacious circling of wagons around the watcher, who dodges sleep in the knowledge of its deception: "Someone must watch, it is said. Someone must be there." At least one person knows that deceit is the law of the night. Deeply lost in the night, the subject is immersed in fictions and narratives that are supposed to make it believe that mattresses, sheets, and blankets offer protection from the cold earth and sky.[110] But someone must brave the wasteland. At least one person watches

　　　　　　　　　　　　　　MARCUS STEINWEG

over god's death. You could interpret this as a negative confession of faith. God is dead; now everything depends on remaining loyal to him by not beginning to believe in him again.

MISUNDERSTANDING

What matters isn't knowledge or experience. It's learning that knowledge exists only as the experience of one's own lack of knowledge.

UNDER SUSPICION

Appeals to "nature" and "the natural" come under suspicion of essentialism, and for good reason. But who is doing the suspecting and on what authority? Routine, unreflective anti-essentialism has long been a symptom of active non-thought. It can be found at every university. You could speak of a vulgar Derrida-ism: a posture that invokes Derrida's deconstruction, and which Derrida would have been the first to repudiate. To claim the inheritance of deconstruction, if there is such a thing, means repudiating this deconstruction that is lacking complexity, and which, in complete contrast to Derrida's, divides the world into good and evil, correct and incorrect. It is a massive theoretical and practical regression. You can learn from Derrida to reject this sort of regression into facile binaries. That's what's demanded by a mode of thought that operates beyond good and evil, and also beyond the alternative between a clear and a guilty conscience. There is hardly a more ideological level than that of conscience, whether you connote it theologically with god or psychoanalytically with the superego. Politically responsible thought can't invoke the authority of conscience or general propriety or an imaginary good. The "true" anti-essentialism places itself under question. Deconstruction is self-deconstruction. It wrests us away from the quietism of unsuspecting suspicion.

LOGOS

The "nude"—according to Platonic–Plotinic tradition—is "the epiphany of the Logos,"[111] writes François Jullien. Isn't it the other way around? In truth, isn't logos the epiphany of the nude, insofar as the nude marks the prelogical real, while logos marks its first formalization in the form of speech and meaning? Before we go making it into the Latin *ratio*, maybe logos isn't much more than the node of extra-rational reality, the point at which its nakedness therefore appears. In that light, it would yield the index of the bare— that is to say, meaningless—existence of the world instead of functioning as the guarantor of its meaning. As the epiphany of the nude, logos indicates an exterior or the real that resists rational inscription. Hence its originary madness. The madness of the activity called thought lies precisely in witnessing the original disjointedness of the thinking subject. At its beginning, the naked real persists. To bear witness to it, to experience it as directly as possible, and to document it is what we might call philosophy.

MARCUS STEINWEG

TWO KINDS OF INNOCENCE

The first consists of freeing yourself from guilt. It spurns any responsibility. Ultimately, it's not about guilt and innocence, but about irresponsibility and self-victimization. The second innocence stands in opposition to the other. It dives into subjectivity as carefree as a child. In that sense, it is like Nietzsche's *innocence of becoming*, which includes the blind affirmation of the world in its ontological indifference. Thus, it does the groundwork for possible responsibility. But the responsibility at stake is beyond all established scales and measures. Responsibility in the horizon of god's inexistence means knowing not what you do. The second innocence also entails having the courage to do it anyway.

UNTIMELY

To fall out of time when you're in the middle of it, by falling into it like a foreign object, is a sign of what Nietzsche calls the *untimely*. As we know, Deleuze associated the untimely with a becoming that skimmed history—including its causality and linearity—in order to churn up its contents by causing the new and unexpected. People who regressively, anachronistically, or sentimentally cling to the past are not untimely. To be untimely means to release the self's grip on the past as well as the present. The untimely destabilizes all possible presences by jutting into them from the future— like an alien or a monster. Thinking implies the willingness to welcome demons and ghosts as friends.

DRUGS

Drugs ensnare us in the dubious fantasies of freedom and creativity. They themselves are a fantasy, and like all fantasies, their evidence clouds our judgement. Badiou sees a sort of metaphysics in them. They distance the subject from established realities, even as they connect it to those very realities. By unshackling pleasure ("la drogue désentrave le jouir"[112]), they shackle the subject to it. In drugs, the fantasy of unshackling collides with the reality of being shackled. In them, a true dialectic of freedom and lack of freedom expresses itself. It's not enough to associate drugs with present-day nihilism as Badiou does. It's not that simple. Drugs intensify the subject's relationship to itself and to the world by identifying it with the emptiness inherent in the self and its world. They heighten the connection to that which it has long been connected to. They show the subject the inconsistency of its realities, and at the same time they show it the way out of its fog of reality, in order to show it the fog-like nature of its consistencies. One fantasy compromises the other by mutually limiting each other. The war on drugs is also always an expression of the paternalistic anxiety of conservative authorities that drugs might seduce the subject to renounce its belief in authority. This is why we can speak of freedom as a nonreligious drug. Freedom isn't what the established powers offer under that name. Freedom is the drug that promises to free the subject from the selling out of freedom.—which makes it as necessary as it is dangerous. After all, what's more menacing than a subject who believes in a promise whose one aim consists in freeing it from all promises?

CARICATURE

We call an exaggerated portrayal a *caricature*. The Latin roots of this word remind us of an overladen cart (*carrus*). Caricaturists overdo it. They take "too much of a good thing" to make a statement beyond the good and the right and the just, which emerges only through this distortion. The caricaturist's satirical and graphical accuracy is the result of systematic overshooting and misfiring. Only in that way can it hit the target. Thus, caricature exemplifies the act of any kind of thinking that consists in reaching *the truth* on the condition of its contemptibility, brokenness, absence, and unavailability.

SEX AND POLITICS

"The apolitical form of contemporary politics"[113] lies not only in the dominance of the economy and the reduction of the political to politics. It is also expressed in a sort of polit-hysterical self-depoliticization through the politicization of everything with a clear, "left" conscience. "If everything is political, then nothing is anymore."[114] To hold on to the political, we must always resist this self-depoliticization. Paradoxically—though it's only ostensibly a paradox—this is possible only if we reconcile politics to its limitations and accept that not everything can be signified and controlled through it. There are zones of the nonpolitical whose preservation contributes to the rescue of the political. That doesn't mean that there are domains that are untouched by political structures, signifiers, and determinants. It means that in the midst of the politicized field that is our reality, they persist as gaps and barriers. They confront the political will with its limitation. There is no love that expresses its relationship only to societal, cultural, and sexual dispositives. In the element of its factual affectation, love is what generates a minimum of distance from these dispositives—not as the romance of its detachment from the world, but rather as the lived defense of an intimacy that is conscious of the fact that it is cemented in the dominant narratives of love, together with the social dependencies defined by them: love as consciousness of a dependency that can be escaped insofar as it can be recognized and laughed at. The zones of the nonpolitical are zones of excessive humor. Far from representing islands of paradisiacal innocence, they are cells of resistance against all imperative narcissistic self-depoliticization. The same goes for sexuality. On the one hand, it is the privileged space of political-ideological conflicts. It is simultaneously a domain of withdrawal and a refusal to be implicated in these conflicts, in order to bend the political scales of value that threaten to suffocate it. Sex is more than the symptom of its underlying cultural-historical dispositive. It refuses its own causality. That makes it the arena of a politics beyond politics. In sex, the subject politicizes itself through temporary depoliticization.

MARCUS STEINWEG

WASTELAND

The fact that humanity leaps from the past like a wounded animal doesn't mean that it escapes it. Jumping out of the old into the new confirms the former as the shore of the latter. It's a leap into the unknown that succeeds if the subject jumps back to the shore to experience it as the true ocean of inconsistency. The past is fragmentary and incoherent. Not even alienation is reliable. No island remains. No childhood comfort. No memory that isn't an illusion. No word that doesn't lie. There is nothing but a wasteland, indistinguishable from the indifference of the sea. The fact that the sea is "at once the symbol of the impossibility and the possibility of the event,"[115] as Badiou says, means that it unites the expanses of immanence with the transcendencies that tear it apart. As in the human subject, the horizontal and the vertical intersect on the sea. This is why Deleuze could evoke it as a zone of eruptive vertical unrest. At times it stands for self-explanatory indifference, at other times for aggressive self-interruption. It perpetuates that which is, indicating it as abyss in the process. It is a metaphor for the rift in being—which Lacan calls the *real*, Deleuze *chaos*, Badiou the *event*—as the break with itself in the texture of being. Thus it exemplifies immanent transcendence.

ALLURE

The allure of thought lies in its stimulation by realities whose unreality is food for thought.

EMOTIONAL ATHEISM

In Michel Houellebecq's *Submission* (2015), the protagonist compares the difficulty an atheist would have empathizing with the description of a conversion with the unlikelihood of "someone who has never been in love, someone to whom love is completely alien, taking an interest in a novel all about that particular passion."[116] You could speak of an emotional atheism, which the unbeliever shares with the nonlover. And yet it's unquestionable that emotional atheism—which describes the inability to love god (it's precisely this love that we call belief) as well as the impossibility of loving other people—is the precondition for the possibility of love and belief. Because it's impossible to provide this love, since other people and god as the Other par excellence withdraw from me (to agree with Lévinas and Derrida), there is room for belief and love. This is the space of the undifferentiable concurrence of possibility and impossibility. True belief implies atheism, true love distance from the religion of emotion. Only emotional atheism, which severs the tie between subject and god as well as subject and subject, constitutes the element of belief and love beyond positive religiosity on the one hand, and the narcissistic romantics of love on the other.

TEACHING

The dilemma of teaching philosophy at a university lies in part in the fact that you can't avoid that the students will learn something. That's not a bad thing, says common sense, and for once it's right. And yet, relevant thought begins with the insight into its unlearnable nature! Demonstrating the impossibility of teaching and learning as their own condition should be the minimum goal of the pedagogy of philosophy. Does that happen so seldom because there are only peddlers of philosophy today and hardly any philosophers?

BLOW JOB

They say that Houellebecq isn't a cynic but a romantic. In doing so, they forget that the cynic is a romantic—a disappointed one.[117] Cynicism lives by keeping illusions alive through ridiculing them. Cynicism is a reckoning with the self. Houellebecq upholds fantasies of love by sexualizing it. It's not about the separation of sex and love, nor about their entanglement. It's about showing that in the position of the protagonist, which is connoted as masculine, love articulates itself as sex: "For men, love is nothing more than gratitude for the gift of pleasure."[118] While the (traditional) female position attempts to verify sex with love, in the male position it is reversed. The blow job performed with devotion is considered the ultimate proof of love: "As for her blow jobs, I'd never encountered anything like them. She approached each one as if it were her first, and would be her last. Any single one of them would have been enough to justify a man's existence."[119] Now, is that cynical or romantic? It's honest, as long as what we call honesty is refusing cynical as well as romantic reveries.

PARAPHRASE

It's the most famous proposition from Wittgenstein's *Philosophical Investigations*: "The meaning of a word is its use in the language."[120] Why not risk the following paraphrase: "The meaning of a philosophy is the sum of the resistance generated to it in reality."

RUIN

That thought comes at a cost is one thing; that it's a cost that can drive the subject to ruin is another. In Bataille, Artaud, Klossowski, Roussel, and Blanchot, Foucault saw writer-philosophers who pushed the thing known as reason to its limits. He soon realized that with his formulation of reason, Kant had already articulated a certain exceedance, insofar as it surpasses understanding. The "first courage you must gather when it comes to knowledge and recognition," he would say in 1978, "consists in recognizing what you can recognize."[121] This courage, which draws borders around the subject's capacities of recognition, is accompanied by another courage, that of exceeding the newly drawn borders. It's this double operation that the *Critique of Pure Reason* performs: dissolution of the subject's borders by setting borders, and setting borders by removing them. Throughout his life, Foucault labored on the critical alliance between excess and analysis. It conforms to his conception of thought, in which meticulous empiricism works in cooperation with hyperbolic experience. The ruin

MARCUS STEINWEG

that menaces every mode of thought persists at the core of this conception. It can never rule out abandoning itself to the indeterminacy of a motion that will cause it to lose control of itself. On the contrary: willingness to lose control is proper to it, just like its critical capacities. What Foucault—with or without Kant—calls critique is the exuberance of thought escaping its confinement in existing realities and knowledge dispositives. This escape doesn't occur as a simple analytical cautionary measure. It marks the dynamic of thought as precise excess. That's why for Foucault, thinking always means thinking differently, and living means living differently, and knowing means knowing differently:

> After all, what would be the value of the passion for knowledge if it resulted only in a certain amount of knowledgeableness and not, in one way or another and to the extent possible, in the knower's straying afield of himself? There are times in life when the question of knowing if one can think differently than one thinks, and perceive differently than one sees, is absolutely necessary if one is to go on looking and reflecting at all. People will say, perhaps, that these games with oneself would be better left backstage; or, at best, that they might properly form part of those preliminary exercises that are forgotten once they have served their purpose. But, then, what is philosophy today—philosophical activity, I mean—if it is not the critical work that thought brings to bear on itself? And if it does not consist in the endeavor of knowing how and to what extent it might

be possible to think differently, rather than legitimating what is already known?[122]

For Foucault, the point is never to lock the subject in its faculties in order to regulate it pedagogically. Foucault is never a thinker for whom proportion is important. He's not Aristotle. He's a thinker who reconciles his critical capacities with his speculative blindness in his conception of thought. However, it's a reconciliation that exposes the subject to a ruinous economy of exceeding itself.

PASSIVITY

The term's erotic connotations are evident. Passivity is the passion of being at someone's mercy. The pain it expresses coincides with the desire for successful self-objectification. The subject fuses with its status as an object, in order to become a subject through this fusing in the first place. However, it is neither the subject as self-consciousness, nor a self-transparent cogito. Passivity constitutes an actively self-negating subject. In the middle of this negation flares the affirmation of a selfless body. Passion is the word that unites negation and affirmation of the self at the level of its physicality. Proper to passivity is the experience of the body at the moment when self-control is lost.

VULNERABILITY

Only thought that increases its vulnerability instead of diminishing it has the chance to be more than repetitive opportunism and idiosyncratic ideology.

MARCUS STEINWEG

BONHEUR

Être heureux à la hauteur des douleurs.
PS: "N'ayez pas peur du bonheur: il n'existe pas."[123]

APORETIC PRAYER

Simone Weil described the ecstasy of thought as openness to unknowing, which is why it coincides with a kind of belief. "We must not seek the void. ... We must not run away from it either."[124] In this double endeavor, the subject moves in the face of god, who doesn't show his face and who coincides with the void. Should we speak of mysticism? Why not, since mysticism names what resists naming. Thought as a vector toward a void that cannot be sought because it already persists within the subject. Thought as aporetic prayer. Self-touch as contact with the void inside myself, as a way of feeling along a meaning that dissipates from its inception. Immense, all-inundating void. The subject carries it within itself and swims in it. It is the ocean of nonmeaning, which Weil makes thought border upon. It is an empty loyalty to the void: "It is the void in our sensibility which carries us beyond sensibility."[125] ("C'est le vide dans la sensibilité qui porte au-delà de la sensibilité.") Thought traces the trail of this transgression. It is the index of the belated coincidence of two voids. That makes it close to prayer. But it's a prayer that grasps at nothing.

CIRCUS ACT

As we know, Heidegger connoted *logos* and the ancient Greek verb *legein* with gathering and bringing together, with a certain concentration, while Derrida associated them with the hyperbolic, madness, and an unrectifiable. Are they simply in contradiction? At least it seems clear that the only mode of thought that can approach the complexity of the questions posed implicitly in both of them is one that allows for the compossibility of both attitudes, and which distances itself to the greatest degree possible from the speculative synthesis of orthodox Hegelianism. You can translate *logos* as "speech and reason," but also as "mind and thought." In any case, it's an entity that is neither at peace within itself nor based on itself. Contrary to Hegelianism—to rejoin it preemptively, you could say—Hegel associated his concept of spirit with turmoil and becoming, with the malleability, historicity, and feverishness of the eventful, instead of sub-stantializing it into an unchanging measure. Hegel's dialectic is the point at which Heidegger's *gathering* intersects with Derrida's *dissemination*. You can speak of complex Hegelianism in reference to both, one that is not only opposed to the orthodoxies of the Hegelians but which also occupies an ambivalent relationship to Hegel's work itself. The ambivalence of this relationship expresses itself in the ambivalent compossibility of identity and difference, gathering and dissemination. In speaking of the identity of identity, Hegel sparks the fire of the problem instead of putting it out. Instead of reading him as a metaphysician of pacification and a dialectician of reconciliation, we should interpret his thought—which passes through a number of iterations—as a high-risk circus act. Nietzsche spoke of himself as a dancer. What he didn't want to hear was that Hegel had already balanced on a rope across the abyss of contingency.

CALL

An obituary: calling after the dead, as if you could recall their deaths by calling them up on the other side.

BODY ESOTERICISM

Nothing tastes as good as skinny feels.
—Kate Moss

"A body," states Jean-Luc Nancy, "is corpulent even when it is thin."[126] Corpulence indicates the body's being as a body, its extension in space, its presence and thickness and its weight: "A body is long, wide, tall, and deep: all of this to a greater or lesser extent. A body is extended. On each side it touches other bodies."[127] There are various ways to evade the body's corpulence. Anorexia is one of them. Anorexics intensify contact with their body by doing everything possible to make it disappear. Even when acutely thin, they try to minimize their corpulence to the point of nothing. They work toward the effacement of their corporeal self, in order to assimilate themselves into nothingness. You could speak of a body esotericism that begins to dissolve the body into the air and worships its virtual absence. The body becomes the placeholder for the void it approaches. Kafka's hunger artist follows this trajectory of renunciation of the self through increased contact with the self. The starving person's intense enjoyment corresponds to the fantastic desire to watch oneself die. There's a word for this kind of libidinous self-dissolution. It's called *narcissism*.

HEART

The heart doesn't break and isn't broken. It doesn't stray into reality.

NOTE ON ODRADEK

If—in a sort of comparative hermeneutic undertaking, as Jean-Claude Milner performs in *La puissance du détail* (2014)—you read Kafka's story "The Cares of a Family Man" alongside "Letter to His Father," you can come to the conclusion that Kafka identifies with Odradek.[128] Odradek is Kafka. Is the enigmatic spool of thread that the family man worries about, as it "lurks by turns in the garret, the stairway, the lobbies, the entrance hall,"[129] claiming to have "no fixed abode," and which may or may not be mortal—a synonym for the author? It can hardly be ruled out. It seems nothing can be ruled out in connection with Odradek. His existence is nearly subjunctive. He does exist, there's no doubt about that. But his mode of existence remains uncertain, along with all of his attributes. Despite his relatively

MARCUS STEINWEG

harmless nature, Odradek is an irritation. Or at least he arouses anxiety in the family man: "He does no harm to anyone that one can see; but the idea that he is likely to survive me I find almost painful."[130] You might think that the function of this unusual creature lies in muddling the simplest certainties and evidence, in his resistance to the effort to name him clearly and to pin him down, that is, to control him, whether through means of thought and language, or through physical force. Odradek drills a hole in the texture of established realities. He marks the point of inconsistency in the social fabric by standing in indifference to its rules rather than partaking in it, in order to follow his own rules, which only he seems to know. Kafka had reasons to identify with Odradek—we know from his diaries how important independence and loneliness were to him. And yet a psychologizing interpretation is unsatisfactory because it contradicts the essence of his prose: the insistence on the inexplicability that flouts every mystification and theologizing and constitutes the law of our existence.

RUSSELL

Did Wittgenstein think Bertrand Russell was an idiot because he was?

UNSETTLING YOURSELF

Derrida defined the political and historical task of thought as a confrontation with the prejudices inherent in it.

Deconstruction means pulling the rug out from under your own feet. That's why he could define the "conformist opinion of 'good conscience'"[131] (Nietzsche spoke of the "fat contentment of the good conscience"[132]) as the enemy of thought. As if the point of politics was to be on the "right side"! Really it's the opposite: being political means refusing the conformism of the good and the right by ceaselessly destabilizing your own axioms, together with the hypotheses and judgments that form their framework. Deconstruction means unsettling yourself.

CAREERISM ON THE LEFT

Opportunism and conformism have slipped to the left because the left moved right—without noticing!

WRITING

In "To Write in a Foreign Language," Etel Adnan compared the act of writing with breathing: "My own writing," she says, reminiscing in this text, which originally appeared in English in 1984, "was like my own breathing: something I was doing."[133] Writing as breathing, writing that has the same evidence as breath. Maybe you could add that writing also entails a certain amount of breathlessness. Writing should have the naturalness and necessity of the breath that keeps the subject alive. The subject resists the thought of a life without writing. We often hear authors say that they couldn't live without writing. Maybe what they mean by that is: I live to write, and I write to live/survive. The nexus of life and writing is the index of their reciprocity and their conflict.

REDUCTION

There are many books that reduce Hegel's thought to Hegelianism—the dialectical machine and its reductive violence—but very few (the best) demonstrate that his reduction to reductionism is an error.

ENERGY

Prior to its ecological considerations, the question of energy is the topos of the subject's general economy. Just like the subject's relationship to itself, its relationship to the world is a complex reciprocal interaction. It involves the investment of energy and its excess. Bataille recognized the principle of sovereignty in the loss of energy.[134] Sovereign subjectivity—its thinking and acting—is a question of energy. Instead of saving energy, it wastes it. The subject only comes to itself through overexpenditure, which annuls the law of reciprocity and equivalent exchange. But it doesn't come home. The economy of waste drives it out of its self-presence, exposing it to the experience of estrangement that has long been its reality. Often, the subject has the tendency to dwell on identity fantasies and idealizations of home instead of affirming being outside of itself. To be sovereign is to affirm going beyond the self. With this affirmation, Bataille embraced the subject-nature of a subject whose subjectivity consists in the lack of subjectivity. It's not economical to invest in a way that is efficiency obsessed, skimping on expenditures. Economic intelligence demonstrates itself in the willingness to play a game whose payout remains doubtful because it is attempted.

THRESHOLD

The fact that works of art "linger on the threshold"[135] of marketing themselves, as Walter Benjamin writes, means that they only do so because they long ago crossed it, and that they are resistant to the market out of grief at their own affinity to the market. Instead of undoing what has been done in order to simulate their integrity, this resistance affirms their factual corruption as the signature of their contact with the world.

PREY

"When I write, philosophy is fertile soil, a humus. I can make use of it," says Heiner Müller in *Krieg ohne Schlacht*.[136] The same goes for politics and conversations overheard on the train. All of that is material.[137] Isn't that also true of philosophy? That it also ranges through ideas, daily life, and cultural history like a hungry animal in search of prey? Thinking means hunting, following others' trails in order to incorporate their concepts and ideas. That doesn't happen without pretentiousness, misunderstandings, violence, and

MARCUS STEINWEG

arrogance. A certain hubris is the condition for thought to be possible. Or at least there is no philosophy that can spare itself this presumption. Its history can seem to be one of unjustified depredation. But it's not about being just. It's about appropriation, assimilation, transformation—making use of things, as Müller puts it.

NOTE ON RORTY

In a work that originally appeared in German, *Die Schönheit, die Erhabenheit und die Gemeinschaft der Philosophen* (1999), Rorty takes measure of the "line between the beautiful and the sublime,"[138] which marks the difference between the conditional and unconditional, finite and infinite, between understanding and reason (as defined by Kant), evoking the conflict between immanence and transcendence. Within the horizon of Hegelian thought, this conflict is mirrored in the formulation of the *identity of identity and difference*, which Heidegger ponders as "togetherness" in "The Principle of Identity" (1957). Undoubtedly this all-encompassing identity isn't just a single one, standing in simple opposition to difference. It itself is difference, which is why you could just as well speak of a *difference of identity and difference*. Applied to the immanence–transcendence conflict, it indicates that there is a tension within the conflict that binds just as it divides. While jejune idealism indulges in the fantasy of a transcendence that emerged from immanence and which is freed from it for good, it is the mark of naive realism to insist on an immanence that has been cleansed of all traces of transcendence. Both attitudes are one-dimensional absolutizations of the conflict, which lag behind Hegel's thought. The task of thought must culminate in the rejection of idealism and realism, in the invention of a heightened realism, which, instead of hastily banishing transcendence from the field of immanence, understands it as the index of the field's lacunae. Transcendence saves immanence from totalization. Far from representing a theological entity, it is the name of the irreducible inconsistency in the space of consistency known as immanence in this case. And so instead of distinguishing between "two kinds of thinkers"[139] and having them collide irreconcilably—the thinker in the mode of the beautiful (immanence, homogeneity, commensurability, consistency, identity) on the one hand, and the thinker in the mode of the sublime (transcendence, heterogeneity, incommensurability, inconsistency, difference) on the other—the aim is to analyze the nearly inseparable intertwining of the two dimensions. Rorty also ultimately recognizes this by calling philosophy the thing that "keeps the tension between these two positions alive."[140]

RIFT

One of the pithiest statements from Luhmann's *Social Systems* (1987), "The system asymmetricizes—itself!"[141] can be paraphrased as a definition of the subject: "The subject asymmetricizes—itself!" In Luhmann, the theories of self-referentiality and of the distinction between system and

MARCUS STEINWEG

environment allow autopoetic systems' relation to the world to be registered as internal asymmetry, which is no objection to their self-referential closure, since it is constitutive for them. It's no different for the subject. The subject is also a self-referential system whose contact with the exterior doesn't represent a self-contradiction. The subject is what borders on a non-external exterior, rather than interiority opposed to exteriority. You can interpret its self-asymmetricization as the index of its ecstasy, a state that had always come over it and didn't only just befall it a posteriori. The subject's self-asymmetricization depicts it as an entity standing in opposition to itself. To recognize that its essence lies in the suspension of essentiality doesn't represent a regression into simple essentialisms. Viewed ontotopologically, the subject is the site of the impossibility of its essence. Luhmann's claim that "the theory of the subject would have to orient itself to the closure of self-referential systems, with the consequence that it couldn't think anymore of anything that does not appear as meaning,"[142] means above all that it must seize nonmeaning constitutively instead of conceiving of it as external to itself. But that means that it owes its closure to an inner rift that Hegel posited as the abyss of negativity.

FINANCE IDIOCY

You have to be an idiot to trust evidence whose consistency is based on promises from idiots who trust that idiots will trust them.

THEATER

Philosophy is theater. You don't understand a philosophical text if you misunderstand its dramaturgy. It's always based on the staging of concepts and ideas. That's why Foucault can speak of "the stage of philosophy," then go on to mention Nietzsche as a philosopher in whose work "the relation between philosophy and the theatre is once again put to occidental philosophy in all its sharpness."[143] The birth of tragedy from the spirit of music is evocative of the birth of philosophy from the spirit of theater. We shouldn't be misled by theater's "condemnation by Plato"; the inaugural moment of philosophy, though perhaps it wasn't a *clear-cut* beginning, represented a theatrical event that is illustrated in the Platonic theater of ideas as staged in the *Politeia*'s Allegory of the Cave.[144] Nor can criticism, of theater as of every philosophical theatricality, escape the temptation of dramaturgy. How could it be otherwise? Is philosophy really concerned with the biggest and emptiest concepts? How can a mode of thought that passes through knowledge (*episteme*) and opinion (*doxa*), reality and appearance, meaning and nonmeaning, jumping restlessly from here to there as if it can't decide where it belongs, not be dramatic? The subject hardly knows what it is speaking of when it says "truth" or "freedom," which makes it the stage of originary fragmentation. Not even when it says "I" can it escape the drama of its mask-like character and self-alienation. Sometimes it stages its life as a tragedy, sometimes as a comedy, by wearing itself out on its contingent high points and dramatic showdowns. "To distinguish between the real and the

MARCUS STEINWEG

illusion, between truth and falsehood," states Foucault, "this is the task of philosophy. The theatre completely ignores these distinctions. There is no sense in asking if the theatre is true, if it's real, if it's an illusion or if it's a pack of lies. ... To accept the non-difference between the true and the false, between the real and the illusion, that's the condition for theatre to function at all."[145] The history of philosophy demonstrates itself to be the "theatre of truth and falsehood."[146] Instead of being a confrontation with theater, which it occasionally was and is, philosophy presents itself as theater performance. That's why it can't avoid theater, because it can't escape its theatrical aspirations. Wherever a stage is erected, the scene opens on the subject's confrontation with its passions and inconsistencies. There is no scene in which it does not appear, fragmented. The stage of thought will remain indebted to the theater of a subject that performs its fever, its lack of orientation, and its indifference in the face of an inaccessible, masked, or in any case inconsistent power. The desire to stage "the theatre of truth"[147] implies the courage to recognize what we call the truth is an entity just as unstable as it is seductive, one that the subject—inside and outside of the theater, if there is an outside—reflects back as director and performer of its realities.

REASONABLE?

Insufficient faculties of thought aren't expressed as insanity, but rather in thought that doesn't recognize its own insanity and calls it reasonable.

DIALECTIC

"In Adorno's philosophical premises, in his theory of the identifying concept, there remains a remnant of that compulsion to identify that he criticizes in philosophical tradition," writes Albrecht Wellmer,[148] and he's right. But there's a problem here. Adorno's achievement lies in having complicated classic dialectic through its substitution by a negative one. From that point on, dialectical thinking is one that constantly turns against itself instead of availing itself of synthesis. The famed claim that "the concept can transcend the concept"[149] says just that. Adorno's *Negative Dialectics* culminates in a critique of identifying thought. It problematizes the reductive violence of the concept. It doesn't do so in order to shift into a nonconceptual or non-identifying mode of thought (insofar as he is still concerned with thought, which is doubtful). The dilemma of a great part of Adorno's reception lies in its misjudgment of the implications and consequences, which is to say the significance, of his dialectical concept. Dialectical thinking is against self-thinking thought. It has nothing to do with moralistic pedagogy. It opposes it nearly diametrically. But it doesn't keep its gloves on. Adorno is operating in contaminated territory. His loyalty to those philosophers he treats critically, such as Kant and Hegel, is a demonstration of this. It makes him a philosopher and distinguishes him from critics: the knowledge that his critique must be paid for with affirmation.[150] Like every anti-idealistic thinker, he's aware that his thought costs him something. Thinking for free is only for those who

MARCUS STEINWEG

don't think. The history of philosophy is the history of problematic credit agreements. Philosophers take out their first
loan from their opponents. Adorno owes Hegel (and others)
significant characteristics of his dialectic—as if he were
financing his invective at least in part from the position
he is arguing against. Dialectical thinkers are those who
recognize these critical credit relationships as the reality of
thought.

SUCCESS

What limits and disenchants any kind of success, and con-
veys its inconsistency and unattractiveness, is its occur-
rence. That is, success is nothing but success!

BOREDOM

Heiner Müller places it at the beginning. Artistic production
comes from boredom: "The main question is how do
you deal with boredom. After a while nearly every state,
whether social or private, becomes boring. Hence our need
for pathos and romance."[151] Today these circumstances are
reversed. To evade romantic pathos, we meet it with boredom. In the political register, boredom takes the form
of lack of imagination; in the aesthetic register, it takes on
critical inoffensiveness with a clear conscience. Neither of
these alternatives is innocent. Both are poorly considered.
You can learn from Müller that innocence isn't an option—
not in this world. Active nonthought, whether in the form

of romantic-emotional or critically inoffensive narcissism, is still a denial of thought and reality. Should you respond to boredom with boredom, with judgment of all thinkable intensities and radicalities? Should you melodramatically exploit them? But isn't the point rather to recognize, in judging and cannibalizing, forms of self-depoliticization that eschew confrontation with aporia and inconsistency, that demand artistic formulation because they belong to our world? Pathos and romance hardly exist except as kitsch. Lack of imagination and inoffensiveness are strategies for systematically blocking out reality. There's a third way, which, rather than a middle road, represents the only radical option: confrontation with the human and extrahuman real at the level of ontological complexity; incommensurability and resistance without indulging in their romanticization, discursive contestation, or homogenization. Those would be the minimal demands on thought as well as on art.

CIRCLE

Going in circles means not getting anywhere. You move without making any progress. Following the circle proves to be a standstill. The subject finds itself in a motionless dynamic. We're accustomed to speaking of closing the circle. The end becomes a new beginning. The subject circles its emptiness by spinning around. Theologically, this means that it is greeting an absent god. To orient oneself toward the absent is to affirm an inexistence that makes all of the

MARCUS STEINWEG

structures of reality into floating architectures. Whether "Jewish or Christian," writes Georges Didi-Huberman, "the absent never ceases its effect, never ceases to demand that humans retain their bond to it. What we call 'art' also serves that purpose."[152] What we call art also rouses us to release ourselves from the absent by affirming its inexistence as the condition for the possibility of a newly invented truth instead of a preexisting meaning. God is dead—that means that the subject is given the chance to straighten itself in the growing wasteland. In circling the void left by god's death, the subject arrives at itself as at something alien. Its contact with itself is contact with the alien. In self-alienation, it meets itself. The circle does not close in order to complete itself. It indicates a different center that the subject must deal with. To welcome instead of resisting a possible form, the void, which has long belonged to it—that is thought, as long as thought means orienting yourself on your lack of orientation.

PERFECTIONISM

Perfectionism is narcissism.

EXCESSES OF REASON

While Adorno affirms the compossibility of artistic exaggeration and critical social analysis, Foucault investigates the "monstrous marriage of literature and madness,"[153] and Derrida asserts the hyperbolism of the cogito and therefore of philosophy, the academicization of theoretical and artistic thought seeks to free reason from its madness at the cost of the loss of reason, as if it were possible to imagine logos without its excess. Ultimately, there are two opposing excesses: the excess of restrictive reason and the excess of the reason that rebels against this reason. Georges Bataille described their difference as that between a restricted and a general economy. They're not equivalent. The first clings fast to the status quo, is politically fainthearted, and tends to be reactionary, while the second extends itself beyond its abilities by refusing to come to terms with established realities. Reasonable reason differs from quibbling reason in that it isn't exhausted by reality.

EVENT

Instead of interpreting the event as vertical transcendence, we should understand it as immanence's break with itself. Immanence is fragmentary. It generates the event as implicit collapse. Anyone who claims to be able to transform fantasies of transcendence into pure immanence reproduces the idealism of the vertical in the horizontal. It's precisely this interplay of horizontal and vertical that suggests the interweaving of immanence and transcendence. Instead of being pure transcendence, the event marks the dramatic effect of this interplay. Immanence rubs against itself like two tectonic plates, generating a quake whose shocks are the effect of immanence, indicating the fragmentary nature of the texture of reality. To put it in Lacanian terms: instead of

MARCUS STEINWEG

representing a naked exterior, the limit of the representable, the real is a product of reality, insofar as it never coincides with itself. Although we're accustomed to thinking of reality as a coherent whole, the fabric of reality is neither self-contained nor identical with itself. It's not just that the real emerges from reality as a product of its breach of self; what we call reality is equally a consequence of the factuality of the real. Immanence results from transcendence, insofar as we understand transcendence as the ontological inconsistency of immanence.

MANET

What Michel Foucault notes about Manet's painting—that it favors the generation of a depth of image over the affirmation of surfaces, which causes what is depicted to recede, two dimensional, behind the presentation of the canvas that bears the image—correlates to the dynamic of desubstantialization in post-Nietzschean philosophy of the twentieth century up to today. This amounts to an attempt to construe the substance (*idea* or *essence*) as a derivative of its materiality. The loss of the anterior world, which the formulation of god's death describes, corresponds to the extension of *this* world, where the subject reconciles itself with its finiteness. Essentially, it's one single world with no way out: a world without a second world. Now everything depends on pursuing the invisible and infinite in the space of heightened visibility and finiteness. That is precisely what Foucault calls thought.

CRISIS

Crises are high points that we experience as low points.

FEELING

The fact that feelings follow conventional narratives rather than expressing an authentic interior doesn't mean that they dissolve completely into ideology. Feelings are emotions that follow patterns in order to play with them. Therein lies their capacity to be critical of ideology: in their deconstruction, as playful as it is aggressive, of the form they take on. There are no feelings that are not opposed to themselves. Love, for example: it hardly exists except in the form of questioning itself. Am I in love? I must be, since I don't know!

UNSPECTACULAR

"Philosophy is perhaps the thing that everyone practices,"[154] says Jean-Luc Nancy, demonstrating an understanding of philosophical practice that emancipates books from books and philosophers from philosophers, opening them to uncertainties, which are irrefutable, insistent, and in that sense also universal and unspectacular.

BACHMANN WITH MÜLLER

There are two sentences that must be read together: The first is by Ingeborg Bachmann: "A work of art doesn't argue."[155] The second is by Heiner Müller: "You can only gain experience blindly."[156] When Müller speaks of experience, he also means the experience of art. He resists the notion that art comes from knowledge. He doesn't say that reflection has no part to play in artistic production. What he means is that the interruption of reflection and the suspension of knowledge is part of experience—that is, blindness. The fact that I don't see anything for a few moments means that something unexpected and new is happening. The new is the disappointment of the old. It's too new to be the continuation of the old into the present. That makes it irreducible to what has passed or to what exists. That has nothing to do with idealism. It implies the differentiation between the conditional nature of experience or the work of art and the negation of its conditions, which cannot be confused with being unconditional. The unconditional is an idealistic fantasy. The suspension of factual conditionality doesn't deny conditionality; it simply suspends its authority. That is the moment of the deauthorization of what exists. Suddenly the subject has no arguments and opens itself to an aporia that can hardly be invalidated.

TRUTH

The "central experience" of writing poetry—and doubtlessly, also philosophy—is supposed to lie in the "margin between truth and its transmission"[157] according to Giorgio Agamben, as if truth were the name of the untransmittable par excellence. The problematic with this view is that it measures the "object" known as truth by the ideal of how objectifiable it is. A progressive conception of truth must free itself from this ideal by indicating something other or more than just its unsuitability for exchange. Instead of standing in opposition to transmission, truth is the name for the margin between the impossible object and the attempt to objectify it. That makes the truth into the real of reality, to put it in Lacanian terms. Truth isn't the failed object of poetry or thought, but rather the reality of this failure as every subject's normality. There is no concept that is less sublime or mysterious. The truth is what was always present: the ontological inconsistency of the subject and its reality.

WHY ALEXANDER KLUGE?

Because he views our world unflinchingly and with curiosity instead of judging it moralistically.

TROPICS

Although the process he called deconstruction—which hardly seems like a practicable method—seems like the essence of hesitation itself, Derrida didn't hesitate to attribute a tropic aspect to thought in general, the sort that earns the name: "tropic, meaning turning, like the spiraling of a turn or a torment."[158] Here he says it in an homage to Jean-François Lyotard. But it applies to thought as such, however singular and distinctive its form might always be. Thought is tropic if it doesn't hesitate to break with its hesitancy, to inflame itself against itself. Feverish tropic thought runs hot and cold. A winding flow of thought that turns back on itself. A flood of ideas, rising, falling, then rising and falling again. In precisely this sense it is "subversive," as Derrida notes: "a movement that revolves, evolves, revolutionizes, overturns from the bottom up." A motion that stays in motion, that is. No mobility, no restlessness— no thought! Restlessness's modes of specification are decisive; the economy of the fever, if you can put it that way, the calibration of its curve. The tropic subject is not yet at the point of turning against its most stable certainties. Prepared to entrust itself to an uncertain future, it turns to the unknown. You could call it romantic and adventuresome— or speculative. But there is no mode of thought that isn't hyperbole itself. Nothing unnerves academic discourse more than the existence of a mode of thought speeding out of the system of facts. That's why thinking has increasingly established itself within academia as the culture of deceleration.

NOTE ON SARTRE

In his book on Sartre, Peter Bürger points to the compatibility of "postmodern thought" and philosophical thought. "Sartre's deep mistrust of interiority"—however much it remained within the horizon of the phenomenology of consciousness—is to be found again anew in Foucault and Derrida, as well as in Deleuze:

Had anyone taken a closer look, ties between Sartre and his postmodern successors were clearly discernible. Instead of faulting his philosophy of the subject in the name of post-modern critique of the subject, hidden continuities in twentieth-century French thought could have been pursued. That's because the subject that Sartre sketches out doesn't moor itself to substantialities of any nature; rather it defines itself as the continuous migration into the future. The critique of self-presence that Derrida presents in lingual-philosophical arguments is already insinuated by Sartre within his philosophy of consciousness. What Derrida describes as the sliding of the signifier happens in Sartre as consciousness sliding out of itself.[159]

By allowing existence to precede essence, Sartre posits a subject without (dictating) subjectivity, or, as Bürger writes, a "subjectivity without identity." It's an originary non-originary subject whose lack of ultimate programming leaves it to wander the desert of incommensurable freedom. What Sartre means by freedom is anything but an idealistic fantasy. Freedom indicates the lack of substantial codification. Sartre proves to be an anti-essentialist or constructivist philosopher, insofar as what he concedes to humanity as essence must be produced by it or at least lie within its sphere of its responsibility. And as much as he tries to relegate Sartre to the nineteenth century, the Foucault of *The Care of the Self* and *The Aesthetics of Existence* reconciles himself to him in a constructivist context: "The hope expressed in these late texts that it must be possible

MARCUS STEINWEG

to devise new forms of subjectivity, which he himself was unable to specify further, finds anticipative fulfillment in Sartre's concept of a subjectivity without identity."[160] In any case, it's an attitude in which the ego or the self and the subject approaches itself "in a relationship of externality." Of course, Hegel, Nietzsche, and Heidegger are precursors to this self-transcendence of the subject, its ecstasy and its exaltation. As long as you view Freud's psychoanalysis together with its category of the unconscious as a discourse of interiority, like Sartre and Foucault, you'll meet it with resistance. Lacan's psychoanalytical thought, on the other hand, can regenerate the subject because it handles the subject of the real as one at odds with itself. As far as Deleuze goes, Agamben was right to point to the significance of Sartre's "transcendental field" in *The Transcendence of the Ego* (1936) as a sort of prototype for the field of immanence.[161] As always in the history of thought, influence and dependence play a tremendous role. They constitute the subject's externality. We could speak of nature or history, together with their cultural, economic, and sociopolitical structures, or of the media and its materiality. A materialist concept of freedom will always be the subject's starting point and its element in the subject's involvement in the existing. Sartre's relevance rests on his freeing the concept of freedom from the idealistic form it had been given. Sartre freed freedom—Lacan, Deleuze, Foucault, and Derrida can't deny it.

DOUBTING DOUBT

"Works of art," writes Martin Seel, "break with the orderliness of our most stable foundations. They remind us that there is no safety even the safest of things."[162] Does that mean that experiencing a work of art is always unsettling, just as the experience of thinking implies the destabilization of the thinking subject? Without a doubt! But who would doubt the evidence and necessity of unsettling the self, and of breaking with the foundational regime? Who would doubt the certainty that we must ultimately go without certainty? We're all seasoned self-doubters, prepared to label all security as illusory without having the courage to doubt doubt itself, the simple fact that it rests on the undoubted, on a "system of evidence," as Wittgenstein puts it.[163] It would be too nice and too simple to view ourselves as the ultimate doubters, as elementary skeptics, while ignoring the foundation of doubt. To follow Wittgenstein's thought means that we can only afford the comfort of constant self-stabilization at the cost of allowing security and certainty to remain unquestioned. The reward for the self-deconstruction of the doubting self is the perspective it provides into its limits. There are kinds of security that, although they themselves remain unsecured, are the prerequisite for thought's destabilization and unsettling of the self. Ignoring them means falling back into the fantasy of unqualified criticism.

MARCUS STEINWEG

RIVALRY

Rivalry is conflict among equals, whereas competition effectively feeds on inequality. Competition seeks to express hierarchy and is motivated by vanity, jealousy, and resentment. Rivals recognize each other as peers. Rivalry is the lived experience of difference in the medium of recognition. That's why there can be rivalry in love and friendship, but never competition.

EVERY WHICH WAY

If anti-intellectualism is the anti-intellectual's love of nature, then intellectualism is the intellectual's love of culture.

BODY

The fact that what we call life does not include dead material can't conceal the fact that it proliferates within the living, as if death mushroomed within life, which led Friedrich Kittler to speak of the "fathomless depths of the body."[164] Agamben is right—he riffs here on a statement from Derrida's *Spectres de Marx*—that the question of life—*What is life?*—plunges the thinking of "our culture"[165] (that is, Western culture) at least into the greatest of difficulties. Maybe this question is exemplary of the aporetic condition of all thought that abandons empirical description as well as formal logical deduction in order to turn to metaphysical problems. It is insufficient to fall in with the usual condemnations, dismissals, and deconstructions of meta-physics and ontology in order to elude the experience of the body's dizzying depths. With the body, through it, the human subject is connected to its animality as well as the experience of exceeding it. The body proves to be the theater of thought. The dust of dead stars swirls and accumulates within it, the memory of dead material, the history of its genetic disposition. The living body, it would seem, before it sets about thinking or reflecting consciously, demonstrates itself to be the archive of humanity, as fathomless as it is fragmentary. It stretches far beyond the human—which remains one monstrous dimension—into ancient unconscious material. In it, the forgotten as well as the never-remembered aggregates. Instead of being merely the museum and the ruin of a history of consciousness, it exhibits the unconscious and never-conscious of this history. It exposes what the memory of the species has evaded. But it's a piecemeal and encrypted exposition of dark particles of matter. With the question of the body, the subject addresses the question of its obscure past. We can call it fathomless because it stretches into the abyss of memory, which is the abyss of thought, a depth that remains bottomless.

NOTE ON NIETZSCHE

In 1861, the seventeen-year-old Nietzsche wrote a school assignment on Hölderlin, in which he defended the poet by invoking his luminous moments, wrung from "the

MARCUS STEINWEG

advancing night of madness." This didn't keep his teacher from advising him "to stick to a healthier, clearer, *more German* poet."[166] Nietzsche wouldn't abandon Hölderlin, even if he later increasingly turned to Goethe. In *Human, All-Too-Human* there is a comment titled "The Treasure of German Prose": "Apart from Goethe's writings and especially the conversations with Eckermann (the best German book in existence) what German prose literature remains that is worth reading over and over again? Lichtenberg's *Aphorisms*, the first book of Jung-Stilling's *Story of My Life*, Adalbert Stifter's *St. Martin's Summer* and Gottfried Keller's *People of Seldwyla*—and there, for the time being, it comes to an end."[167] Nietzsche's Goethe-philia is connected to his enthusiasm for Stifter's *St. Martin's Summer* (1857) because he sees the Dionysian wellspring, the nocturnal chaos beneath the surface of form and idylls, signaled instead of suffocated. This is why Walter Kaufmann could claim that the concept of the Dionysian in the late Nietzsche represents the alliance of Dionysus and Apollo, which Nietzsche legitimated in defense of the "Dionysian faith of Goethe."[168] If we associate the categories of light and dark or day and night with the opposition of Apollo and Dionysus, then it's insufficient to see them reflected in the difference of Weimar classicism, with all of its possible variations of "dark romanticism" (including Hölderlin and Kleist). The difference gets lost in the heart of this position, as it articulates the dialectic of light and dark without exception. Perhaps dialectic—in its Platonic and Hegelian variations, from Heidegger's primal struggle between *lethe* and *aletheia*, hiddenness and unhiddenness, to Adorno's negative dialectic—is always concerned with the conflict between evidence and lack of evidence, day and night, the visible and the invisible.

METHOD OF IMMANENCE

Among the rare moments when Foucault speaks of love—instead of passion, desire, and sex—is this one:

> Maybe we should also say that in love we sense how the body closes on itself. Finally ·it exists beyond all utopia, with all of its density, in the hands of the other. As the fingers of the other wander over your body, all of its invisible parts begin to exist. Your own lips become perceptible on the lips of the other. Before the other's half-closed eyes, your own face attains definition. Finally there is a gaze capable of seeing your closed lids. Like mirrors and death, love also assuages the utopia of the body, allows it to fall quiet, calms it, shuts it in a box more or less, which locks and seals it away.[169]

In love, lovers supposedly experience a little relief from the "mania" of the body, which consists of the fact that it "is constantly decaying and dissipating." Love is capacity for coherence, in that it gathers the body's dispersion and lacking unity into a closed form. For moments at a time, the body seems like an intact entity. The illusory power of love makes the subject feel that its body is identical with itself. They may

MARCUS STEINWEG

be brief moments, like flashes of light whose experience-ability is beyond doubt, in which the utopia of the body yields, along with its earthliness and reification. You could speak of love as a method of immanence, which answers the transcendence of the utopian with insistence on the presence of the beloved's body here. And so instead of viewing (romantic) love as nothing but escapism, it can be interpreted as a method for coping with utopia. The other—the other's gaze, caresses, erotic demands—generates the space for an experience of immanence that allows the subject to be here, now. It doesn't wallow in narcissistic fantasies and stereotypes. On the contrary: love frees the subject from its romantic self-distance by short-circuiting it—and, for the moment at least, reconciling it—with its concreteness. Not every reconciliation is delusory, indicating idealism, glorification, and metaphysics. What Foucault posits as love is overcoming the utopia of the body in favor of a topos that orients it on its immanence instead of its transcendence. The locking and sealing that he speaks of is the precise opposite of the narcissistic-romantic self-closure of transcendence fantasies. It's a kind of contact with the other that bursts solipsistic egoism apart instead of confirming it. Love entails an experience of otherness that calms and soothes. It lets the subject—during moments of passionate encounters—be what it is: a body that is open to another body, which is a substitute for it—beyond the fantasy of merging together. No fixed identity or unity restitutes itself during the encounter. It verifies the naked fact of being a subject without a given identity.

SECOND-ORDER ILLUSION

Adorno's claim that the "illusion of purity"[170] is inherent in intellectual production—that is, its exemption from the material-economic—has long slipped into general consciousness to the point that the first and nearly exclusive expectation on art, literature, theater, and philosophy is to exhibit and reflect impossible purity, which in turn leads to the illusion of pure impurity, to the insistence that the claim to autonomy is nothing but a reflex of factual heteronomy, which—in the horizon of Adorno's aesthetic theory—is true only if the noncontradictory nature of heteronomy and autonomy is recognized, insofar as the former forms the basis for the possibility of the latter.

FOR NO REASON

I love, speak, act, and think—for no reason! Is that true? Hardly! I have thousands of reasons. What I'm missing is *the* reason.

WINDOW

A window is different from a door, in that you open and close it without passing through it.

DEPTH

The fact, as Blanchot notes,[171] that Foucault had little affection for the concept of depth doesn't mean that he indulged in simple affirmation of the surface. On the contrary: together with Nietzsche, Foucault gave depth to surfaces and lent their lightness a weightless weight.

LEFT

Why can I only imagine being on the left as uncomfortable? I simply can't warm up to the idea of a comfortable way to be on the left. For me, being on the left means being uncomfortably opposed to the right, the dogmatic left, and myself. People on the left never have any peace. Not even in their own perception and self-conception.

LOVE'S LIE

Romantic love entails its imitation. We know this from Stendhal and Flaubert, as René Girard reminds us: a lie persists in the heart of love.[172] To love does not mean loving authentically. True love loves love's lie. Loving means lying. The subject lies to the beloved other as to itself by attesting to the authenticity of its love. If you love, you want to be loved. Loving means making a pact with love's lie in order to make people believe you're not lying. If there's something like authentic love, it implies the affirmation of its inauthenticity by reflecting its motivation. There is no simple contradiction between lying and loving. People who love convincingly gather the courage to admit to its lack of genuineness. Does that mean that they only pretend to love? It means that the lover risks everything on loving at the level of the compossibility of lying and loving. The dishonest thing about love is that the loving subject can love along stereotypes that repudiate its spontaneity. Its intimacy expresses itself through imitation. Only in the emulation of romantic dispositives of love can love exist. But it's not enough to abandon oneself to narcissistic fantasies in order to blindly affirm them as Emma Bovary does. Instead of pulling back from love's lie, love demands stepping into it purposefully. Love neither leads to the subject's complete objectification through the ideology of love, nor does that ideology express an autonomous subject. It's much more banal than the classic narratives of love would like to admit: in love, the subject experiences that it is bound up in realities that it can escape by recognizing their power over it.

NOTE ON RACISM

In the chapter of *The Ground of the Image* (2003) titled "Image and Violence," Nancy comes to the topic of the relationship between violence and racism. After he declares violence to be "profoundly stupid"—"stupid in the strongest sense, the thickest and most irremediable sense. It is not the stupidity that comes from a lack of intelligence, but much worse: it is the stupidity of the stupid twat [*con*]. It is the calculated absence of thought willed by a rigid intelligence," he goes on to say of racist violence: "It is violence that knocks someone in the face, simply because—as the stupid twat might say—it 'doesn't like the look' on this face."[173] The crucial thing about this remark, which imitates the vulgar affect of racist brutality, is that it posits racism (of which there are only violent varieties) as a problem of thought in the form of its absence rather than one of stupidity. Racism is first an error of thinking made by people who do not think, which then emerges as an opinion—with an ever uglier face—in which the refusal to think manifests itself as a robust insanity. When it comes to the most elementary and in this sense unconditional, if not also ahistorical, recognition of the other as an equal subject, the point is not the exchange of opinions but rather the refusal to think, as long as thinking is understood here to mean accepting evidence of equality between subjects of differing origin as a matter of course, instead of giving in to the resentment that is at work in all forms of racism, the fear of equality that threatens the supposedly free sectionalism of opinion. Racism feeds on the feeling of being threatened by the non-exclusivity of a community of equality, which accepts every subject as subject *per definitionem*. You're a twat if you do everything you can not to think, in order to arm yourself with your fear and stylize yourself as a victim. Thinking means demonstrating its own subservience, arbitrariness, and inconsistency to the doxa. Since there is no subject that is freed—once and for all—from doxological reaction, thinking always also means to think against yourself, to think further, endlessly further than active non-thought (which Nancy attributes to the stupid twat) wants to consider doing even for a second. A simple and utterly preliminary definition of racism might be: racism is self-victimization before the backdrop of resentment-fueled self-aggrandizement. An error of thinking made by people who do not think!

CREATIO

In *Il fuoco e il racconto* (2014), Agamben says that the act of creation is determined by the "double structure" of two contradictory forces: "élan and resistance, inspiration and critique."[174] That leads him to the basic dialectical experience of artistic—as well as scientific and philosophical—creation. The subject always finds itself in a state of agitation that causes it to fluctuate between impulsiveness and method, haste and stagnation, proflection and reflection. The fire that artists kindle in the heart of established realities must encompass the entire dialectic of agitation, instead of just being the ember of passion. Instead of simply differentiating between the mystery and the story, as Agamben does, we should recognize a flame in their contentious compossibility, which feeds philosophy and science, poetry and art, in that they employ inspiration and critique to the same degree. That's what is meant by the resistant nature of the act of creation: the refusal to sacrifice critique to inspiration or proflection to reflection. Actually, élan and resistance, passion and calculation, excess and precision all go hand in hand. A work of art is moving when it succeeds in uniting both sides, exposing its conflict as well as the difficulties of mediating it. The resistant nature of the act of creation entails the struggle against the idealistic varnishing of its artificial character, its adhesion to

MARCUS STEINWEG

the existing, as well as its belonging in the world. The work is autonomous in that it exposes its heteronomy. It is itself exhibition, even before it is put on display: exhibition of the fire it ignites, exhibition of the means and forms of its articulation—exhibition of its resistance to the normalcy it never stops being a part of.

COURAGE

In Kant's essay "What Is Enlightenment?" (1784), Michel Foucault recognized a "call to courage."[175] The famed challenge—addressed to all of humanity—to emerge from immaturity implies a *sapere aude*: the courage to think, the emancipation from subjection to the thinking of others. Kant is touching on the human ability to become conscious of one's own heteronomy in order to—gradually—free oneself from it. In the context of further considerations that stray from Kant, Foucault spoke of the "courage of the truth,"[176] which is tantamount to his definition of philosophical thought. The courage of the truth turns out to be the courage of thinking. The act of thinking—which includes processuality and interminability—includes working on the truth, "analysis of the relations between the subject and truth: that of relations of power and their role in the interplay between the subject and truth."[177] The courage of truth must question the instrumentalization of the truth and its fusion with established power. Far from dismissing truth as a metaphysical concept—and with and without Kant—Foucault defines the task of his thought as the analysis of the truth. Courage demands this analysis, if only because as a critical project, it cannot trust any simple solutions—as far as the alliance between knowledge and power goes, for example. Strictly speaking, it can't trust anything. The courage of truth is inherent in the tradition of enlightenment not only in the form of a challenge, but also as problem and aporia. You could call Foucault the thinker of this inherence. His entire body of thought expresses consciousness of the aporia of thought concerning the truth. This is why it is thought—because thinking doesn't mean searching for solutions. Thinking means working through problems that elude solvability. Kant was also clear on this. The subject is in a bind. That's what the subject's humanity consists in: being in contact with questions and problems that it can neither dismiss nor solve.[178] And that's what requires courage.

WAR IN PEACE

Before, you had enemies. Today, you're subject to hostilities.

READY FOR FLIGHT

Thinking entails the courage to be carefree in a way that is considered unprofessional in academia. But there is no philosophy beyond speculative flyovers that allow the subject to perceive the loss of the ground under its feet as a chance instead of a danger. Derrida once spoke of Husserl's dogged caution, which reached its limit at the moment when it came into contact with the inconsistencies of its axiomatics.[179] But those are the true moments of thought: moments when control is lost, along with orientation. Thought that refuses to fly isn't thought at all. You misunderstand its dynamic if you see nothing in it besides a secure sequence of steps, the careful weighing of arguments, reflection sheltered by scholarly methodology. Thinking entails recklessness. In the most intense moments of his thought, even Husserl—whose perspective Fjodor Stepun described as that of a "watchmaker gone mad"[180]—was dedicated to the disintegration of his own constructions—for example, when approaching the problem of "passive genesis" and that of the "alter ego," at which point he stood facing the limits of his "system." His diligence couldn't save him from a certain sort of self-deconstruction. The law of every mode of thought finds expression in it: to be exposed to the abyss of its evidence. From this perspective, you would have to associate the entire Hegelian project with constant readiness for flight (which, for example, constantly manifests itself in new system designs). If Kant pronounced a certain flight ban for the subject in order to guarantee its connection to the forms of intuition of space and time, Hegel is the philosopher who lifted this ban in order to define reason as speculative excess. Heidegger expressed this with the realization that speculation became autonomous. It doesn't amount to much more than the articulation of readiness to think, to purchase one's rigor and care at the price of a certain carefree attitude. Constantly being surprised by the new is part of everyday life in philosophy. A statement by Martin Kippenberger applies here: "He who confronts the abyss, should not be surprised if he can fly."

TOTALLY

Overheard on the bus: a dialogue between two girls, one of whom asserts that she's "totally happy!" (Of course, they were talking about love.) If there is a coherency of post-Nietzschean thought, it articulates itself in questioning the idea of totality, which is associated with Hegel's speculative dialectic, with metaphysics, and with successful "absolute knowledge"—whatever you consider that to be. Progressive anti-Hegelianism expresses itself in the insistence on a remainder that is resistant to any desire for totality and consensus. Bataille called it the heterogeneous and Adorno called it the non-identical. From that point on, thought meant being open to irreducible singularity. Does that make philosophers spoilsports who compromise the love fantasies of narcissistic children? Or is the girl on the bus—whose claim of happiness is an example, for anti-Hegelians, of the Hegelian happiness-in-unhappiness dialectic and the metaphysics of pacification—not hot on the trail of a heightened critique of ideology by showing metaphysics-critical negativism the cold shoulder (without even taking notice of it) of unconditional love? The narcissism of the cold-hearted might mean they love without loving, but they do it with the utmost resoluteness. That is, totally!

MARCUS STEINWEG

BIRTH

It's already a narcissistic wound if the child experiences it as a betrayal instead of a promise or an honor—which is why Marguerite Duras could say that it's the next closest thing to murder. Everything that follows becomes a footnote to this wound. The research into its grammar is what Freud called psychoanalysis.

RELIGION OF REASON

Reason cedes its place to the religion of reason at the moment when it begins to struggle against its constitutive excess, replacing it with moralistic rigorism.

CLICHE VERSUS IMAGINATION

In a conversation with Harun Farocki, Heiner Müller once found fault with the "occupation of imagination by clichés"[181] in American Disney movies. Everyone understands what he meant by that. But it's only half the truth. It also works the other way around. In film, as in supposedly real life, clichés are masked by imagination. Thinking always means both: questioning the occupation of imagination by clichés, as well as the analysis of how they are obscured by imagination.

BREAKING AWAY

Like no other, Foucault described the act of thought as "breaking away." When thinking, the subject distances itself from itself and its certainties and realities, in order to embark on an uncharted voyage. "The movement by which, not without effort and uncertainty, dreams and illusions, one detaches oneself from what is accepted as true and seeks other rules—that is philosophy. The displacement and transformation of frameworks of thinking, the changing of received values and all the work that has been done to think otherwise, to do something else, to become other than what one is—that, too, is philosophy."[182] Nothing is more foreign to philosophy than walling oneself in with what already exists. Nothing contradicts it more than the wish to arrive at the self, to allow the subject to be identical with itself so that it can be at peace in the image that it makes of itself. Rather, the point is to increase the restlessness and to allow the number of self-images to mushroom into the incalculable, so that it realizes that one valid image of itself exists only as a Platonic fantasy with an anesthetic or narcotic effect. With Foucault, you have to conceive of philosophy as the practice of unrest, and as the thinking subject's dynamic of self-acceleration. Precisely here, at the increased speed of thought that never comes to a stop, thinking comes into its own. It doesn't reach its home or an ultimate destination or self-coincidence, as conservative dispositives would have it. Rather, it is the (always problematic) identification of the subject with its ontological fever, which robs it of breath—as long as it is thinking.

WITTGENSTEIN

"What I know, I believe,"[183] Wittgenstein believed to know, expressing his certainty of belief as belief in certainty.

DEPRESSION

"I'm so empty," the depressive laments, concealing the fact that their depression disavows the emptiness rather than being its expression, in that it functions as its substitute.

DANCE

Nietzsche didn't just say that Zarathustra was a "dancer." He made the language itself dance, its concepts and dispositive, vocabulary and grammar. What is dancing, if not the willingness to suspend everything gravitational by translating it—rather than fighting against it—into a lightness of motion that is the affirmation of contingency: knowing that things are as they are, without forcing them to be so? In dance, the primacy of the future articulates itself before the present and the past. That is the dancer's abandon: those who dance have nothing to lose but loss. So, absolutely nothing. But they do it with the utmost precision.

ALEATORY

We call something aleatory if it limits chance with coincidence.

THINKING

Now that god is dead—but, as Nietzsche already knew, his death is an unending agony—everything depends on thinking of the incommensurable in the horizon of increased commensurability. But that implies that thinking means dedicating oneself to the rifts in the structure of immanence and the inconsistencies in the fabric of consistency that we call reality. Thinking means losing the ground under your feet.

DIALOGUE

They often say art is dialogue. It's about understanding. Just as often you hear that the only legitimate art is that which resists consensus. Art interrupts the monophony of consensus. It's disruptive, in that it suspends conversation from the start. Once again, it doesn't come down to a simple contradiction. Maybe we can put it this way: art communicates and creates dialogue by questioning communication and dialogue. That doesn't mean that no understanding is reached. But they're dialogues that expand into polylogues, which generate contentious monologues. With just as much justification as you can claim that art is about dialogue, you can say it's about monologue. It would be naive to believe that dialogues aren't polylogic monologues.

MARCUS STEINWEG

DEFINITION

And if, instead of love of wisdom, we were to translate *philosophía* as yearning for the truth?

SHOCK

Why shouldn't we expect philosophy—like art—to shock us? The shock would be the product of disappointed expectation. Suddenly everything would look different. You couldn't even depend on the shock. But that's potentially the source of understanding: that I no longer understand anything at all—only that everything remains to be understood. Nothing would be as it was before.

ESCAPE

It's true that we escape clarity by fleeing into the dark. But this escape also functions in the other direction. Thinking means fleeing the escape in both directions.

THINK AGAIN!

Those who think don't act—think those who act without thinking.

SECOND THOUGHTS

... are what people have who don't think.

FLIES

"What is your aim in philosophy?" asks Wittgenstein in section 309 of his *Philosophical Investigations*, and answers: "To show the fly the way out of the fly-bottle." What if the way out consists in knowing that there isn't one? Maybe the aim of philosophy is to free oneself from the fantasy of a way out. Fantasies are always both the illusion of inescapability and the illusion of escape. Too infrequently does it become clear that inescapability and escape represent imaginary ways out. What people flee is their compossibility. It's not about either inescapability or escape. It's about realizing that inescapability itself is the escape. The aporia of philosophical as well as literary and artistic thought demands that we identify ourselves with the fly in the fly-bottle instead of showing it a way out. This is precisely what Kafka does.

Notes

1. G. W. F. Hegel, *Elements of the Philosophy of Right*, translated by T. Knox (Oxford: Oxford University Press, 1953), 13. Originally published as *Grundlinien der Philosophie des Rechts* (Berlin, 1820).

2. Those who are in pain are extremely in touch with themselves, losing themselves in self-contact and losing contact with the outside through that. The registry of this loss is what Hegel called thought or the labor of the concept.

3. Jacques Derrida, *Artaud le Moma* (Paris: Galilée, 2002).

4. G. W. F. Hegel, *Lectures on the Philosophy of Religion*, vol. 1, edited by Peter C. Hodgson (Oxford: Oxford University Press, 2006), 313. Originally published as *Vorlesungen über die Philosophie der Religion I* (Berlin, 1832).

5. Michel Foucault, *Language, Madness, and Desire*, edited by Philippe Artières, Jean-François Bert, Mathieu Potte-Bonneville, and Judith Revel, translated by Robert Bononno (Minneapolis: University of Minnesota Press, 2015). Originally published as *La grande étrangère: A propos de littérature* (Paris: Éditions EHESS, 2013). Foucault continues: "All in all, you can say that the question 'What is literature?' first reached us with the work of Mallarmé, and that with this event it could be put into words" (ibid.).

6. Alain Badiou, *Sarkozy: Pire que prévu, les autres: Prévoir le pire* (Fécamp: Editions lignes, 2012).

7. It's a mistake to think that contemporary thought has settled into immanence. Thinking is unsettled thinking because it does not allow itself this ease. Though earlier philosophy

seemed to have set the subject on the track of a metaphysics of pacification and happiness-in-unhappiness dialectic, whose collateral was a certain concept of transcendence that assured the existence and consistency of a transcendental signifier, the thought of modernity—and here Hegel is the watershed, half happiness-in-unhappiness dialectician, half sad proto-Adornian metaphysician—found itself ever more rapidly exposed to the inexistence of such an entity. The anti-Platonism as well as the anti-Hegelianism of a large portion of the philosophy of the twentieth century generated this increased unrest of a transcendentally homeless subject who finds no orientation in the desert of immanence other than its own lack of orientation. Now—and Nietzsche essentially already said this—everything depends on not making a new god out of this subject of immanence's lack of orientation: the god of nihilism, or of the last man, which tends toward a religion of immanence. Immanence isn't absolute. It has holes that you can call points of transcendence or inconsistency, as long as these concepts are understood as formal, areligious terms for naming the ontological incompleteness of the fabric of immanence that is our reality. The point is not to reintro-duce transcendence into immanence, as reactionary political and fundamental religious ideologues demand. The point is to show that the substitution of transcendental metaphysics with a religion of immanence remains trapped in the model of seamless continuity and necessity. A "new dialectic between the finite and the endless" (Alain Badiou, *Métaphysique du bonheur réel* [Paris: Presses Universitaires de France, 2015], 10) would have the function of intellectually formalizing the immanence of transcendence, or as Badiou puts it, the "immanence of truths." (*L' immanence des vérités* is the title of the forthcoming third part of the outline of Badiou's math-ematical ontology, together with the 1988 *L'être et l'événement* and the 2006 *Logiques des mondes*.)

8. Derrida says precisely that when he claims in his examination of Lévinas that the phenomenology of the other and of

time implies the questioning of "original self-evidence." See Jacques Derrida, "'Genesis and Structure' and Phenomenology," in *Writing and Difference*, translated by Alan Bass (Chicago: University of Chicago Press, 1978), 205. Originally published as *L'écriture et la différence* (Paris: Seuil, 1967).

9. Martin Heidegger, "Letter on Humanism," in *Pathmarks*, edited by William McNeill, translated by Frank A. Capuzzi (Cambridge: Cambridge University Press, 1998), 293. Originally published as "Brief über den Humanismus," in *Wegmarken* (Frankfurt: Vittorio Klostermann, 1967).

10. Foucault, *Language, Madness, and Desire*.

11. Michel Foucault, *Manet and the Object of Painting*, translated by Matthew Barr (London: Tate, 2012). Originally published as *La Peinture de Manet* (Paris: Seuil, 2004).

12. Michel Foucault, "The Minimalist Self," in *Politics, Philosophy, Culture: Interviews and Other Writings, 1977–1984*, edited by Lawrence D. Kritzman, translated by Alan Sheridan et al. (New York: Routledge, 1988), 12. Originally published in *Ethos* (autumn 1983).

13. Franz Kafka, "Little Fable," in *The Great Wall of China: Stories and Reflections*, translated by Willa and Edwin Muir (London: Secker, 1933). Originally published as "Kleine Fabel," in *Beim Bau der Chinesischen Mauer* (Berlin: Gustav Kiepenheuer Verlag, 1931).

14. Foucault, *Language, Madness, and Desire*, 517.

15. Ibid.

16. Friedrich Nietzsche, *Beyond Good and Evil*, translated by Walter Kaufmann (New York: Random House, 1966), 197. Originally published as *Jenseits von Gut und Böse* (Leipzig, 1886).

17. Rainer Maria Rilke, *Diaries of a Young Poet*, translated by Edward Snow and Michael Winkler (New York: W. W. Norton, 1998), 30. Originally published as *Briefe und Tagebücher aus der Frühzeit* (Leipzig: Insel, 1931).

18. Friedrich Nietzsche, *Thus Spake Zarathustra*, translated by R. J. Hollingdale (New York: Penguin, 1961), 103. Originally published as *Also sprach Zarathustra* (Paris: Ernst Schmeitzner, 1883–1891).

19. Friedrich Hebbel, *Tagebücher 1835–1843*, vol. 1 (Munich: dtv, 1984), 342.

20. Ludwig Wittgenstein, *On Certainty*, edited by G. E. M. Anscombe and G. H. von Wright, translated by Denis Paul and G. E. M. Anscombe (Oxford: Blackwell, 1969), 151, no. 177. Originally published in German as *Über Gewißheit* (Frankfurt am Main: Suhrkamp, 1970).

21. Immanuel Kant, *Critique of Pure Reason*, edited and translated by Paul Guyer and Alan Wood (Cambridge: Cambridge University Press, 1998), 99. Originally published as *Kritik der reinen Vernunft* (1781).

22. This has the consequence, as Žižek says in reference to Badiou, "that philosophy is by definition excessive; that it literally exists only through the excessive connection to external conditions, which are of either an amorous, political, scientific or artistic nature." Alain Badiou and Slavoj Žižek, *Philosophy in the Present*, edited by Peter Engelmann, translated by Peter Thomas and Alberto Toscano (Cambridge: Polity Press, 2009), 69. Originally published as *Philosophie und Aktualität: Ein Streitgespräch* (Vienna: Passagen, 2005).

23. Heiner Müller, *Krieg ohne Schlacht* (Cologne: Kiepenheuer & Witsch, 1999), 298.

24. Badiou and Žižek, *Philosophy in the Present*, 76.

25. Ibid.

26. Hebbel, *Tagebücher 1835–1843*, 340.

27. Narcissistic people experience the incompatibility of their self-understanding with their real self as a painful rift, reacting defensively against reality, since they can only experience reality as a narcissistic wound. Vain people, on the other hand,

trust the congruence of their imago with their factual self in the sociosymbolic structure, dismissing all doubt of this equivalence as imaginary.

28. Slavoj Žižek, *Less Than Nothing* (London: Verso, 2012),151.

29. Jean-Luc Nancy, *Ego sum* (Paris: Flammarion, 1979), 77. Cf. Grünbein on Descartes:

> Descartes was enough of a dialectician to understand that thinking—like loving—follows a certain direction, owing to which it is in a constant state of exchange with all that is not mind, all that is not itself. He was never so exclusively committed to his infelicitous concept of the *thinking substance* that, for all its necessary independence of the body, he wouldn't have also recognized consciousness as action and interaction, as intentional, object-oriented and personal. From the self-experience of consciousness in the most fleeting state of aggregation arose, as if of themselves, all possible varieties of interference and interdependence: penetration by outside influences, distraction, delusion, deliberate blindness, and everything else that was part of the adventures of the living mind.

See Durs Grünbein, *Descartes' Devil: Three Meditations*, translated by Anthea Bell (New York: Upper West Side Philosophers, 2010), 96–97. Originally published as *Der cartesische Taucher* (Frankfurt: Suhrkamp, 2008).

30. Nancy, *Ego sum*, 77. Elsewhere, Nancy says that the Cartesian subject, which is blind to itself, marks the "point of evidence" to an equal degree that it marks the "point of blindness." See Jean-Luc Nancy, *Philosophische Salons*, edited by Elisabeth Schweeger (Frankfurt: Schauspielfrankfurt-Belleville Verlag, 2004), 47.

31. This is why Žižek can speak of "the madness at the heart of Descartes's *cogito*" and of the "constitutive madness of the Cartesian subject." Slavoj Žižek, *Event* (London: Penguin, 2014). See also Slavoj Žižek, *Die Nacht der Welt:*

Psychoanalyse und Deutscher Idealismus (Frankfurt: Fischer, 1998), 10–22; "Cogito and the History of Madness," in Derrida, *Writing and Difference*, 36–76.

32. Friedrich Nietzsche, *Twilight of the Idols*, edited by Michael Tanner, translated by R. J. Hollingdale (New York: Penguin, 1990), 82. Originally published as *Götzen-Dämmerung* (Leipzig, 1889).

33. Theodor Adorno, *Minima Moralia*, translated by E. E. N. Jephcott (London: New Left Books, 1974), 50. Originally published 1951.

34. Ibid., 49.

35. Jacques Lacan, *The Four Fundamental Concepts of Psychoanalysis*, edited by Jacques Alain Miller, translated by Alan Sheridan (New York: Norton, 1981), 29. Originally published as *Le séminaire: Livre XI: Les quatre concepts fondamentaux de la psychanalyse* (Paris: Seuil, 1973).

36. Serge Leclaire, *Démasquer le réel: Un essai sur l'objet en psychanalyse* (Paris: Seuil, 1971), 19.

37. Ludwig Wittgenstein, "A Lecture on Ethics," translated by Max Black, *Philosophical Review* 74, no. 1 (1965): 3–12. Originally published as "Vortrag über Ethik" (1930).

38. Jean-Luc Nancy, *Philosophical Chronicles*, translated by Franson Manjali (New York: Fordham University, 2008), 16. Originally published as *Chroniques philosophiques* (Paris: Editions Galilee, 2004).

39. Jacques Rancière, "Si l'art résiste à quelque chose?" Lecture given at 5th International Philosophical Symposium on Nietzsche and Deleuze: Art and Resistance, 2004, Fortaleza, Brazil.

40. Gilles Deleuze, *Fold: Leibniz and the Baroque*, translated by Tom Conley (London: Athlone Press, 1993), 76. Originally published as *Le pli: Leibniz et le baroque* (Paris: Editions de Minuit, 1988).

41. Jean-Luc Nancy, *The Sense of the World*, translated by Jeffrey S. Librett (Minneapolis: University of Minnesota Press, 1993). Originally published as *Le Sens du monde* (Paris: Éditions Galilee, 1993).

42. Roland Barthes, *The Neutral*, translated by Rosalind Kraus and Denis Hollier (New York: Columbia University Press, 2007), 173. Originally published as *Le Neutre: Cours et séminaires au Collège de France 1977–1978*, edited by Thomas Clerc and Éric Marty (Paris: Seuil, 2002).

43. Franz Kafka, *Diaries, 1910–1923*, translated by Martin Greenberg (New York: Schocken Books, 1948), 222, entry from July 1, 1913. Originally published in German as *Tagebücher 1910–1923* (Frankfurt: Fischer, 1951).

44. Ibid., 229, entry from August 15, 1913.

45. Jacques Derrida, "A 'Madness' Must Watch Over Thinking," in *Points ...: Interviews 1974–1994*, edited by Elizabeth Weber, translated by Peggy Kamuf (Stanford: Stanford University Press, 1995). Originally published as *Points de suspension, Entretiens* (Paris: Éditions Galilee, 1992).

46. On the figure of the expatriate himself in reference to Roger Laporte, see Linda Lê, *Par ailleurs (exils)* (Paris: Christian Bourgois Editeur, 2014), 138–139.

47. "*Ja,* or the *faux-bond* II," in Derrida, *Points ...: Interviews 1974–1994*, 36.

48. Friedrich Kittler and Till Nikolaus von Heiseler, *Flaschenpost an die Zukunft: Eine Sendung* (Berlin: Kulturverlag Kadmos, 2013), 107.

49. Ibid., 19.

50. Heraclitus, *Heraclitus: The Complete Fragments*, translated by William Harris (Middlebury: Middlebury College, 1994).

51. Heiner Müller, *Gespräche 3: 1991–1995* (Frankfurt: Suhrkamp, 2008), 843.

52. Robert Esposito, *Communitas: The Origin and Destiny of Community*, translated by Timothy Campbell (Stanford: Stanford University Press, 2004) 87. Originally published as *Communitas: Origine e destino della comunità* (Milan: Giulio Einaudi Editore, 1998).

53. Michel Foucault, *Religion and Culture*, edited by Jeremy R. Carrette (New York: Routledge, 1999), 111. Originally published as "Sei to kenryoku" in *Gendai-shisô* (Trieste: Edizione Luglio, 1978), and later as "Sexualité et pouvoir," in *Dits et écrits*, vol. 3, edited by Daniel Defert and Francois Ewald (Paris: Gallimard, 1994).

54. Martin Heidegger, "Plato's Doctrine of Truth," in *Philosophy of the Twentieth Century: An Anthology*, edited by Henry D. Aiken and William Barrett, translated by John Barlow (New York: Random House, 1992), 258. Originally published as *Platons Lehre von der Wahrheit* (Bern: Francke Verlag, 1954)

55. Ibid.

56. Ibid., 260.

57. Ibid.

58. Martin Heidegger, *Parmenides*, translated by Andre Schuwer and Richard Rocjcewicz (Indianapolis: Indiana University Press, 1998).

59. Giorgio Agamben, *Infancy and History: The Destruction of Experience*, translated by Liz Heron (London: Verso, 1993), 103. Originally published as *Infanzia e storia: Distruzione dell'esperienza e origine della storia* (Torino: G. Einaudi, 1978).

60. François Jullien, *Vital Nourishment: Departing from Happiness*, translated by Arthur Goldhammer (New York: Zone Books, 2007), 105. Originally published as *Nourrir sa vie: À l'écart du bonheur* (Paris: Seuil, 2005).

61. Nietzsche, *Beyond Good and Evil*, 85.

62. Ludwig Wittgenstein, *The Big Typescript. TS 213*, edited and translated by C. Grant Luckhardt and Maximilian A. E. Aue

(Hoboken, NJ: Blackwell, 2005), 85, no. 423. Cf.: "The complexity of philosophy is not a complexity of its subject matter, but of our knotted understanding" (Wittgenstein, *Philosophische Bemerkungen, Werkausgabe*, vol. 2 [Frankfurt: Suhrkamp, 1984], 9).

63. Ludwig Wittgenstein, *Tractatus Logico-Philosophicus*, translated by C. K. Ogden and Frank P. Ramsey (London: Keegan Paul, 1922), 4.112. Originally published as *Tractatus Logico-Philosophicus*, in *Annalen der Naturphilosophie* 14 (1921).

64. Gilles Deleuze and Felix Guattari, *A Thousand Plateaus*, translated by Brian Massumi (Minneapolis: University of Minnesota Press, 1987), 240. Originally published as *Mille plateaux* (Paris: Les Éditions de Minuit, 1980).

65. Nietzsche, *Twilight of the Idols*, 103.

66. Ibid.

67. Badiou, *Sarkozy*, 75.

68. Ibid., 76.

69. Müller, *Gespräche 3*, 9.

70. Ibid., 294.

71. Martin Seel, *Aktive Passivität* (Frankfurt am Main: Fischer, 2014), 102–103.

72. See Heiner Müller, *Theater ist kontrollierter Wahnsinn* (Berlin: Alexander Verlag, 2015).

73. See: Žižek, *Event*.

74. Jacques Derrida, "Paul de Man," in *The Work of Mourning*, translated by Pascale-Anne Brault and Michael Naas (Chicago: University of Chicago Press, 2001), 75. Published in *Chaque fois unique, la fin du monde*, ed. Pascale-Anne Brault and Michael Naas (Paris: Galilée, 2003).

75. You can also say this with a sentence of Voltaire's often attributed to Giovanni Pico della Mirandola: "Faith consists ... in

believing things because they are impossible." Voltaire, *The Philosophical Dictionary*, selected and translated by H. I. Woolf (New York: Knopf, 1924).

76. Martin Seel, *Theorien* (Frankfurt am Main: Fischer, 2009), 29.

77. Lacan, *The Four Fundamental Concepts of Psychoanalysis*, 15.

78. Wittgenstein, *Tractatus Logico-Philosophicus*, 5.632.

79. Wittgenstein, *Tractatus Logico-Philosophicus*, 7.

80. Ludwig Wittgenstein, "A Lecture on Ethics," translated by Max Black, *Philosophical Review* 74 no. 1 (1965). Originally published in German as *Vortrag über Ethik* (Berlin: Suhrkamp, 1989).

81. Ibid.

82. Ibid.

83. Kant, *Critique of Pure Reason*, 99.

84. "A mode of thought that thinks is always oriented toward what it cannot think," writes Lyotard. See Jean François Lyotard, "François Châtelet, une philosophie en acte," in *Misère de la philosophie* (Paris: Galilée, 2000).

85. Kant, *Critique of Pure Reason*, B310 f., p. 350.

86. Cf. Marcus Steinweg, "Wittgensteins Tier," in *INAESTHETICS 2: Animality*, edited by Wilfried Dickhoff and Marcus Steinweg (Berlin: Merve, 2011), 42–49.

87. For discussion of "The turning of the concept of order into a fundamental paradigm, both metaphysical and political," in which the "reciprocal coordination" of transcendence and immanence is expressed, see Giorgio Agamben, *The Kingdom and the Glory: For a Theological Genealogy of Economy and Government*, translated by Lorenzo Chiesa and Matteo Mandarini (Stanford: Stanford University Press, 2011), 83–84. Originally published as *Il regno e la gloria: Per una genealogia teologica dell'economia e del governo. Homo sacer II, 2* (Milan: Neri Pozza, 2007).

88. François Châtelet, *Une histoire de la raison: Entretiens avec Émile Noël* (Paris: Seuil, 1992), 42.

89. Nietzsche, *Beyond Good and Evil*, 113–114.

90. Michael Hirsch is correct to interpret the "strengthening of the cultural left" as "a symptom of the weakness of the political left." See Michael Hirsch, *Logik der Unterscheidung—Zehn Thesen zu Kunst und Politik* (Hamburg: Textem Verlag, 2015), 9.

91. Slavoj Žižek, *A travers le réel*, edited by Fabien Tarby (Fécamp: Editions Lignes, 2010).

92. See Jacques Lacan, *The Seminar of Jacques Lacan: The Ethics of Psychoanalysis (Book VII)*, edited by Jacques Alain-Miller, translated by Dennis Porter (New York: Norton, 1997). Originally published as *Problèmes cruciaux pour la psychanalyse: Séminaire 1964–1965* (Mantes: Imprimerie mantaise, 1981).

93. Paul Valéry, *Tel quel* (Paris: Gallimard, 1941–43).

94. Gilles Deleuze, *Dialogues II*, translated by Hugh Tomlinson and Barbara Habberjam (New York: Columbia University Press, 2007), 164.

95. Mehdi Belhaj Kacem, *Aprés Badiou* (Paris: Grasset, 2011). See also *Etre et sexuation* (Paris: Stock, 2013).

96. Kacem, *Aprés Badiou.*

97. Ibid., 25.

98. See, e.g., Maurice Blanchot, *L'écriture du désastre* (Paris: Gallimard, 1980), and Jacques Derrida, *Feu la cendre* (Paris: Editions les femmes, 1987).

99. Alain Badiou, *A la recherche du réel perdu* (Paris: Fayard, 2015), 30.

100. Ibid., 37.

101. Foucault, *Language, Madness, and Desire.*

102. Friedrich Nietzsche, *Ecce Homo*, translated by R. J. Hollingdale (New York: Penguin, 1979), 65.

103. Ibid., 86.

104. Wittgenstein, *Big Typescript*, 413.

105. "Sexuality and Power," in Foucault, *Religion and Culture*, 130.

106. Derrida—let us remember—speaks of the "necessity" and "fatality" of "contamination" as "a contact originarily impurifying thought or speech by technology." You could just as well say, by all realities that compromise its auto-projectionist hygiene. See Jacques Derrida, *Of Spirit: Heidegger and the Question*, translated by Geoffrey Bennington and Rachel Bowlby (Chicago: University of Chicago Press, 1991), 10. Originally published as *De l'esprit: Heidegger et la question* (Paris: Galilée, 1987).

107. Hebbel, *Tagebücher 1843–1847*, 326.

108. Theodor Adorno, *Negative Dialectics*, translated by E. B. Ashton (London: Routledge, 1973), 191. Originally published as *Negative Dialektik* (Frankfurt: Suhrkamp, 1966).

109. Franz Kafka, "At Night," in *The Complete Stories of Franz Kafka*, edited by Tania and James Stern (New York: Schocken Books, 1971). Originally published as "Nachts" in *Die Erzählungen*.

110. You can define the sky as a dimension of opening, as Nancy does, while the earth indicates closure (Jean-Luc Nancy, *Au ciel et sur la terre* [Paris: Bayard, 2004], 13–14). Sky and earth would be related to what Heidegger calls world and earth in his essay "The Origin of the Work of Art," interpreting the strife between the two spheres as the conflict between *aletheia* (unhiddenness) and *lethe* (hiddenness). As we know, Agamben's thought moves within this dispositive (and not without complicating it). The decisive question is how to think of an unilluminated darkness—as earth or sky or world? One possible answer is to declare it a point of inconsistency in the

contingent totality of being. The fact that there is earth means that the finiteness of the sky is threatened by the infiniteness of a closure that is the condition for the possibility of an endless opening.

111. François Jullien, *The Impossible Nude: Chinese Art and Western Aesthetics*, translated by Maev de la Guardia (Chicago: University of Chicago Press, 2007), 92. Originally published as *De l'Essence ou Du nu* (Paris: Seuil, 2000).

112. Alain Badiou, *Images du temps présent: Le Séminaire 2001–2004* (Paris: Fayard, 2014), 58.

113. Jean-Luc Nancy, *The Creation of the World or Globalization*, translated by François Raffoul and David Pettigrew (Albany: SUNY Press, 2007), 108. Originally published as *La création du monde ou la mondialisation* (Paris: Galilée, 2002).

114. Nancy, *Philosophical Chronicles*, 25.

115. Badiou, *Images du temps présent*, 418.

116. Michel Houellebecq, *Submission*, translated by Lorin Stein (New York: Farrar, Straus & Giroux, 2015), 37. Originally published as *Soumission* (Paris: Flammarion, 2015).

117. See the worthwhile book by Aurélien Bellanger, *Houellebecq écrivain romantique* (Paris: Editions Léo Scheer, 2010).

118. Houellebecq, *Submission*, 25.

119. Ibid., 25–26.

120. Ludwig Wittgenstein, *Philosophical Investigations*, edited by P. M. S. Hacker and Joachim Schulte, translated by G. E. M. Anscombe, P. M. S. Hacker, and Joachim Schulte (London: Blackwell, 1953), 42, no. 43. Originally published as *Philosophische Untersuchungen* (1953).

121. Michel Foucault, "Qu'est-ce que la critique?" *Bulletin de la Société française de philosophie* 84, no. 3 (1990).

122. Michel Foucault, *The History of Sexuality*, vol. 2, translated by Robert Hurley (New York: Random House, 1985), 8. Originally

published as *Histoire de la sexualité II: L'Usage des plaisirs* (Paris: Gallimard, 1984).

123. Michel Houellebecq, *Rester vivant, et autres textes* (Paris: J'ai lu [Flammarion], 1991), 21.

124. Simone Weil, *Gravity and Grace* (Lincoln: University of Nebraska Press, 1997), 68. Originally published as *La Pesanteur et la Grâce* (Paris: Plon, 1947).

125. Ibid., 69.

126. Jean-Luc Nancy, *58 indices sur le corps* (Montreal: Éditions Nota bene, 2004), no. 4.

127. Ibid.

128. Jean-Claude Milner, *La puissance du détail: Phrases célèbres et fragments en philosophie* (Paris: Grasset, 2014).

129. Franz Kafka, "The Cares of a Family Man," in *The Complete Stories*, translated by Willa and Edwin Muir (New York: Schocken Books, 1995). Originally published as "Die Sorge des Hausvaters," in *Die Erzählungen*.

130. Ibid.

131. "Heidegger, the Philosophers' Hell," in Derrida, *Points ...*, p. 184.

132. Nietzsche, *Twilight of the Idols*, p. 54.

133. Etel Adnan, "To Write in a Foreign Language," in *Unheard Words*, edited by Mineke Schipper (London: Allison & Busby, 1985), 117.

134. See Georges Bataille, *Inner Experience*, translated by Leslie Anne Boldt (Albany: SUNY Press, 1988). Originally published as *L'expérience intérieure* (Paris: Gallimard, 1943).

135. Walter Benjamin, "Paris, the Capital of the Nineteenth Century (Expose of 1935)," in *The Arcades Project*, translated by Rolf Tiedemann (Cambridge, MA: Harvard University Press, 1999), 13. Originally published as "Paris, die Hauptstadt des XIX.

Jahrhunderts," in *Das Passagen-Werk* (Frankfurt: Suhrkamp, 1983).

136. Müller, *Krieg ohne Schlacht*, 271.

137. "The material is random. It washes in by chance," says Müller. See Müller, *Gespräche 3*, 425.

138. Richard Rorty, *Die Schönheit, die Erhabenheit und die Gemeinschaft der Philosophen* (Frankfurt: Suhrkamp, 2000), 16.

139. Ibid., 35.

140. Ibid., 40.

141. Niklas Luhmann, *Social Systems*, translated by John Bednarz Jr. and Dirk Baecker (Stanford: Stanford University Press, 1996), 38. Originally published as *Soziale Systeme: Grundriß einer allgemeinen Theorie* (Frankfurt: Suhrkamp, 1984).

142. Ibid., 516.

143. Michel Foucault, "The Stage of Philosophy," in *New York Magazine of Contemporary Art and Philosophy* 1.5, https://web.archive.org/web/20110520222341/http://www.ny-magazine.org/PDF/The_Stage_of_Philosophy.html (accessed June 1, 2016). Originally published as "La scène de la philosophie" in *Dits et écrits*, vol. 3.

144. You could also speak of a "shadow theater" as Han does. In Byung-Chul Han, *The Transparency Society*, translated by Erik Butler (Stanford: Stanford University Press, 2015), 37. Originally published as *Transparenzgesellschaft* (Berlin: Matthes & Seitz, 2012).

145. Foucault, "The Stage of Philosophy."

146. Ibid.

147. Ibid.

148. Albrecht Wellmer, *Endgames*, translated by David Midgley (Cambridge, MA: MIT Press, 1998), 258–259. Originally published as *Endspiele: Die unversöhnliche Moderne. Essays und Vorträge* (Frankfurt: Surhkamp, 1993).

149. Adorno, *Negative Dialectics*, 9.

150. Derrida summarized the relationship between critique and affirmation as follows:

> The *critical* idea, which I believe must never be renounced, has a history and presuppositions whose deconstructive analysis is also necessary. In the style of the Enlightenment, of Kant, or of Marx, but also in the sense of evaluation (esthetic or literary), *critique* supposes judgment, voluntary judgment between two terms; it attaches to the idea of *krinein* or of *krisis* a certain negativity. To say that all this is deconstruction does not amount to disqualifying, negating, disavowing, or surpassing it, of doing the *critique of critique* (the way people wrote critiques of the Kantian critique as soon as it appeared), but of thinking its possibility from another border, from the genealogy of judgment, will, consciousness or activity, the binary structure, and so forth. This thinking perhaps transforms the space and, through aporias, allows the (non-positive) affirmation to appear, the one that is presupposed by every critique and every negativity. ("A 'Madness' Must Watch Over Thinking," in Derrida, *Points ...*, 357)

151. Müller, *Gespräche 3*, 432–433.

152. Georges Didi-Huberman, *L'Homme qui marchait dans la couleur, sur James Turrell* (Paris: Minuit, 2001).

153. Michel Foucault, "La folie et la société," in *Dits et écrits 2: 1976–1988* (Paris: Gallimard, 2001).

154. Jean-Luc Nancy, *C'est quoi penser par soi-même ?* (Paris: Editions de l'aube, 2015), 16.

155. Ingeborg Bachmann, *Essays, Reden, Vermischte Schriften*, vol. 4 (Munich/Zurich: Donauland, 1978), 112.

156. Müller, *Gespräche 2*, 412.

157. Agamben, *Infancy and History*, 147.

158. "Lyotard and Us," in Derrida, *The Work of Mourning*, 222.

159. Peter Bürger, *Sartre: Eine Philosophie des Als-ob* (Berlin: Suhrkamp, 2007), 12–13.

160. Ibid.

161. Giorgio Agamben, "Bartleby, or On Contingency," in *Potentialities: Collected Essays in Philosophy* (Stanford: Stanford University Press, 1999).

162. Martin Seel, *Theorien* (Frankfurt: S. Fischer, 2009), 131.

163. Wittgenstein, *On Certainty*.

164. Friedrich Kittler, *Das Nahen der Götter vorbereiten* (Paderborn: Wilhelm Fink, 2011), 45.

165. Giorgio Agamben, *The Open: Man and Animal*, translated by Kevin Attell (Stanford: Stanford University Press, 2004). Originally published as *L'aperto: L'uomo e l'animale* (Turin: Bollati Boringhieri, 2002).

166. See Walter Kaufmann, *Nietzsche: Philosopher, Psychologist, Antichrist* (Princeton, NJ: Princeton University Press, 1974), 23.

167. Friedrich Nietzsche, *Human, All-Too-Human*, translated by Paul V. Cohn and Helen Zimmer (New York: Dover, 2006), 400. Originally published as *Menschliches, Allzumenschliches* (Paris: Ernst Schmeitzner, 1878).

168. Kaufmann, *Nietzsche*, 323.

169. Michel Foucault, *Les Hétérotopies: Le Corps Utopique* (Fécamp: Editions Lignes, 2009), 19.

170. Adorno, *Minima Moralia*, 133.

171. Maurice Blanchot, *A Voice from Elsewhere*, translated by Charlotte Mandell (Albany: SUNY Press, 2007). Originally published as *Une voix venue d'ailleurs* (Paris: Gallimard, 1992).

172. René Girard, *Deceit, Desire, and the Novel: Self and Other in Literary Structure*, translated by Y. Freccero (Baltimore: The Johns Hopkins University Press, 1965). Originally published

as *Mensonge romantique et vérité romanesque* (Paris: Editions Bernard Grasset, 1961).

173. Jean-Luc Nancy, *The Ground of the Image*, translated by Jeff Fort (Bronx: Fordham University Press, 2005), 16, 17. Originally published as *Au fond des images* (Paris: Galilée, 2003).

174. Giorgio Agamben, *Le Feu et le récit*, translated by Martin Rueff (Paris: Rivages, 2015), 53. Originally published as *Il fuoco e il racconto* (Rome: Nottetempo, 2014).

175. Foucault, "Qu'est-ce que la critique?"

176. "Le courage de la vérité" is the title of Foucault's last seminar at the Collège de France in 1983–84. See Michel Foucault, *The Government of Self and Others*, edited by A. Davidson, translated by Graham Burchell (New York: Palgrave Macmillan, 2008). Originally published as *Le Courage de la vérité: Le gouvernement de soi et des autres* (Paris: Seuil, 1984). See also Frédéric Gros, ed., *Foucault: Le Courage de la vérité* (Paris: Presses Universitaires de France, 2002).

177. Foucault, *The Government of Self and Others*, 8. The "first courage you must gather when it comes to knowledge and recognition," he continues, "consists in recognizing what you can recognize" (59).

178. Cf. Sartre: "Man is the being through whom questions come into the world; but man also is the being to whom questions come into the world that concern him and that he cannot resolve." Jean-Paul Sartre, *Truth and Existence*, translated by Adrian van den Hoven (Chicago: University of Chicago Press, 1992). Originally published as *Vérité et existence* (Paris: Gallimard, 1989).

179. See Derrida, *Points ...*, 88.

180. See Hans-Georg Gadamer, *Philosophical Apprenticeships*, translated by Robert R. Sullivan (Cambridge, MA: MIT Press, 1985), 35. Originally published as *Philosophische Lehrjahre* (Frankfurt: Vittorio Klostermann, 1977).

181. Heiner Müller, *Gespräche: 1965–1987* (Frankfurt: Suhrkamp, 2008), 164.

182. Michel Foucault, "The Masked Philosopher," in *Michel Foucault: Politics, Philosophy, Culture,* edited by D. Kritzman, translated by Alan Sheridan (New York: Routledge, 1988), 330. Originally published in *Entretiens avec Le Monde, I, Philosophies* (Paris: Le Découverte/Le Monde, 1984), 21–30.

183. Wittgenstein, *On Certainty.*

Printed in the United States
by Baker & Taylor Publisher Services